the music biz meets the personal computer

START ME UP!

the music biz meets the personal computer

START ME UP!

by Benjamin Krepack and Rod Firestone

foreword by Joe Walsh

START ME UP!
(the music biz meets the personal computer)

Book Design by Patti Podesta
Cover graphic by Patti Podesta and David Bleiman
Illustrations by Marv Newland

Published by Mediac Press
P.O. Box 3315
Van Nuys, CA 91407
(818) 904-0515

1st Printing — May 1986

Printed in the U.S.A.

ISBN 0-9616446-0-5

Library of Congress Catalogue Card Number: 86-60846

Contents

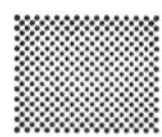

CHAPTER 4 - PLANNING IT OUT 43

CHAPTER 5 - HITTING THE ROAD 61

CHAPTER 6 - THE PROMOTION & PUBLICITY GAME 87

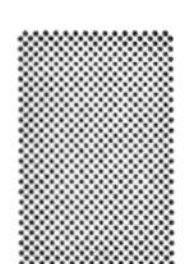

ACKNOWLEDGMENTS

We'd first like to thank everybody who took time out of their busy schedules to talk to us about their work, their lives, and their computers. We're particularly indebted to Bobbi Cowan, Derek Sutton, and Janet Ritz for their advice, encouragement and contacts. We'd also like to express our appreciation to Don Singleton, Neil Quateman, and Steve Mendell at IMC, Roger Powell of Cherry Lane and Utopia, Perry Leopold at PAN, Tom Seufert at Red Wing Studios, Larry Linkin of NAMM, David Cooper at Fox Productions, MicroTimes Magazine, and Gerald Rafferty.

We owe Marv Newland, ("Bambi Meets Godzilla"), of International Rocketship Limited, a load of thanks and kudos for the time, talent, and imagination he put into his great drawings we've used to start up each chapter.

Of course, our very special thanks go to Joan Welch and Julie Weissman for their love, support, patience, and meals. Joanie also helped in the editing process and we thank her for her time and feedback.

Finally, thanks to our families and our friends for promising to buy this book.

Benjamin Krepack and Rod Firestone
April 1986

FOREWORD

Ah, yes! Time marches on. Technology, however is starting to run. So, what's the forecast for the future? Methinks some good news and some bad. The bad news being that mankind may well end up working for the very technology orginally created to serve it. The good news is that we have computers.

I remember when we didn't.

True story: When I was very young, I went with my parents to visit a friend of theirs who was an "audio engineer". I remember talking with him about this new thing he and these other guys had been working on. He played a tape of a train (a locomotive, by the way). It was very loud and there were two speakers — not just one like everybody had back then. I remember being scared because it seemed like the train was coming right through the living room. I even looked out the window to see if I could see this train as it disappeared to the east. I remember him saying, "We're going to call what you just heard 'stereo' and it's going to change recorded music from now on."

Another true story: I have been a "ham" radio operator since 1962. I used to listen to the old-timers talking late at night about some guys they knew who had discovered a way to replace tubes and that these guys had decided to call whatever they had discovered "transistors". They were saying that this "solid-state" approach was the key to the future of modern technology — especially in a field they were calling "electronic logic circuit design," which is what computers were born from. There were computers back then (maybe two), but a slide rule was just about as fast, a lot more dependable, and a good twenty to thirty thousand dollars cheaper.

Now today, I strongly oppose all the computerized video games — either in arcades or for "kids" to entertain themselves at home. The all-time Donkey Kong high score just doesn't impress me very much. There are much better investments — even at 25 cents a shot. I worry that five years from now, anybody under 17 will be able to land the space-shuttle and defend some lunar base from an evil asteroid attack, but the wonderful world of literary folks like Mark Twain and others will be replaced by some coin operated video screen fiction with no plot. I even worry that five years from now, no one under 17 will be able to read.

The human brain has two separate sides — roughly equivalent to this: one side is digital, the other side is analog. In other words, one side can read and the other side can think about what was read. One side can work a word processor, the other side can tell the hand to write things on a piece of paper. One side interprets the time-of-day from a digital watch which says13:02, the other side recognizes that the hands of a clock are saying that it's 2 minutes after 1.

This book deals with both sides of the human brain. One side is reading these words, and the other side will, hopefully, translate what is being read into a better overall understanding of what the relentless future has in store for us.

I would stress that this book deals with peaceful applications of computer technology. Like any good book, it will stimulate your imagination. Mark Twain would approve. The rest is up to you. Enjoy.

With great hopes for the future....

Joe Walsh
April 1986

Introduction

ABOUT THIS BOOK

Computers in the music industry? It almost sounds like a contradiction in terms. Isn't the music business supposed to be one of the "people" industries, where it's not what you know, but who you know? Well, the answer is yes. And no.

Yes, the business is a "people" business and always will be. The industry, as a whole, thrives on talent, instinct, and imagination, all things that you can't get out of a computer — at least not yet. Nevertheless, a lot of people in the music industry are using computers in their work — and that's sparking a technological revolution that is changing many of the old standards, rules, and practices of the business. This book is about the revolution.

Who's This Book Written For?

Whether your status in the music industry is that of professional, amateur, apprentice, student, rookie, veteran, or dreamer, this book is for you. Here, in no particular order, is a list of some of the people who can benefit from the information in this book:

- musicians/songwriters
- record companies
- business managers
- recording engineers
- record distributors
- journalists
- road managers
- tour accountants
- tour truckers
- video directors
- video producers
- record producers
- music fans
- personal managers
- record company execs
- record promoters
- publicists
- music industry attorneys
- concert promoters
- production managers
- music publishers
- roadies
- lighting and sound
- booking agents
- disk jockeys
- radio program directors

What Will You Get Out Of This Book?

That really depends on how much you already know about the music industry and how it operates, and about computers. A young, self-managed musician struggling on the local music scene in New York, Nashville, Los Angeles, San Francisco, London, or any other city would probably get an incredible amount of new information from this book — not only about the new technology of the business, but also about the unique responsibilities of managers, agents, promoters, and other professionals. While a seasoned music industry pro, who already knows all about how the business functions, could learn a lot about the technological advances that are changing the way things are done in his or her field.

Our primary purpose in writing this book wasn't to define the inner-workings of the music business. What we set out to do was to illustrate and explain the industry's use of computers in an easy-to-understand, non-technical manner. By reading this book, you'll familiarize yourself with computers and learn why they are playing such a significant and expanding role in virtually every facet of the music industry. But that's not all. We'll also clue you in on how professionals in the industry are using computers right now, and how people will be using computers even more in the future. We'll take you backstage, on the road, in the offices, and over the telephone lines to show you how computers are turning the music industry into an even more efficient and profitable enterprise. If you're trying to break into the industry you'll be in a better position to get the job you're after, and if you're already working in the industry, you'll be better equipped to advance in your music business career.

We'll also give you some sound advice and practical information on computers in general so that you can confidently "talk shop" with computer sales people, consultants, and users. Besides lowering the risk of being "fast-talked" into purchasing a system that you don't need, this information will help you overcome what is commonly referred to as "techno-phobia" (the fear of unfamiliar technology). It's a disease we all suffer from now and again. We hope that this book is one of the cures.

Keeping Up With The "State Of The Art"

It's impossible to write a non-fiction book without the constant fear that the material will be dated and somewhat obsolete by the time the book hits the stores. This is particularly true when it comes to books about computers. New technological developments happen so fast that even the weekly trade periodicals have trouble keeping up. Trying to capture high-tech information in book form is tough. It's like trying to take a picture of a speeding automobile with an Instamatic camera. You'll still be able to tell it's a car, but the picture will be blurry, unfocused. This is one of the reasons we decided not to make any specific recommendations about what computer hardware or software you should buy. At the current rate of change, today's modern miracle could easily become tomorrow's old hat.

Another reason we aren't recommending one computer over another is that, as with most things in life, what is good for one person is not necessarily good for another. Each person and each business within the music industry has unique needs and different styles and methods of working. So, instead of advocating one particular system, we discuss many different kinds of computers. We believe that this approach will help you feel more comfortable about computers in general, and that you'll then be able to make your own educated and knowledgeable decisions about which computer is right for you.

How Is This Book Organized?

Probably the biggest challenge in writing this book was deciding how to organize it. We wanted to remain true to our initial goal of writing a book for people in the music industry who don't know that much about computers. But having found so many people in the industry using and understanding computers, we finally came up with an approach we felt good about: In the text portion of each chapter, we've dealt with how computers can be and should be used in the industry. Then, we've complemented each chapter with real-life industry examples. These "Connections" will put you in touch with a variety of professionals in the music business who use computers in their daily lives.

Photographs, computer screen simulations, drawings, and cartoons are used to illustrate some of the products, terms, and concepts brought up in each chapter. Because we used two Macintosh computers to write this book, many of the program examples and screen pictures are taken from Macintosh products. The disproportionate number of Macintosh-related illustrations is born out of convenience (and the fact that the Mac lends itself to graphic illustration better than any computer we know of). But we don't want you to interpret this bias as an endorsement of the Mac. We feel that a piece of word processing, spreadsheet, database, or communications software is basically the same animal on any brand of computer.

Now and then you might come across a music or computer term that you don't understand. Any term that you find italicized can be found in the Glossary located in Appendix A. We've also included a section called "Quick Answers To A Few

Frequently Asked Computer Questions" in Appendix B. The information in these two appendicies won't make you a computer expert, but they will help you understand many of the buzz words, concepts, and common terminology associated with computers and the music business.

Appendix C is a compendium of music industry and computer resources that may be helpful if you need more information on any subjects discussed in this book. Included here are lists of hardware and software manufacturers, computer and music trade publications, information networks, consultants, and other related services.

Take It Away

Even if you've had some experience with computers, you will get a lot out of the information provided between these covers. But, as we said before, this book is truly written for people who are uninitiated in the world of computers. If you have never even touched a computer before, don't worry about it. We'll start you up.

Chapter One

WORKING IN THE OFFICE

"There's no business like show business." Right? Wrong. The music business is, in fact, just like all other businesses in that there's still a product or a service to push. And, that means letters to write, information to file, contracts to sign, people to pay, and a lot of other work to do from a desk.

Whether you're running your business in an office or out of your home, a small computer system can help you get your act together in ways that you've probably never dreamed possible. No matter what you do in the music business, a computer system can help you get organized and stay organized.

This chapter is for everyone and anyone who's doing anything in the business. Whether you're part of a large, international record company, or a musician managing your own career, you have correspondence or material to get out and files to maintain.

Computers have been helping people do these things in the typical office setting for years, and right now there's a terrific selection of versatile computer systems to choose from. A small and unassuming desktop computer available today can do the same job that it took a roomful of large machines to do just ten years ago.

Anybody Wanna Buy a Typewriter?

Let's talk first about getting out nice, clean, professional-looking correspondence. Of course we're talking about *word processing*. If you're unfamiliar with the benefits of word processing, you're in for a big surprise. If your operation is small and you don't have a secretary, word processing could save your life. If you do have a secretary, word processing *software* may make your office run so much more efficiently, that your support staff will finally be able to get onto those other projects that there never seems to be time for. Many people find that the word processing capability alone justifies the investment they've made in a small computer system. This is especially true when you consider the high cost of a decent electric typewriter.

Software for word processing is designed with the understanding that people never manage to write what they want to say the first time they try. A word processor allows you to change the words, the format, and the entire look of whatever it is you're composing — as many times as you want — *before* you ever commit it to paper.

If you happen to have someone who does the typing for you, word processing will allow you to type up the first draft and then let your typist worry about the format, grammar, spelling, and punctuation. Typists love word processing because it means they don't have to retype a whole letter or document every time someone changes it.

Copies of documents are very important in our business, especially when you use letters to confirm agreements that you may have made over the telephone. With word processing software (and your computer and *printer*), it's easy to generate as many copies as you might need. Plus, you always have a copy saved on your *disk.*

Or let's say you have ten letters to get out, all of which need to say essentially the same thing. With word processing software you only need to write that common information once. After that, you can go into each individual letter modifying and personalizing it as necessary.

It's also easy to create form letters that can be used — and modified— again and again.

Suppose you've just moved to a new location and you need to notify all the hundreds of people that you do (or would like to do) business with. Without a word processor, you would probably type up a simple announcement and use a salutation like "Dear Sirs" or "To Whom it May Concern." Then you would make as many copies as you needed on a copy machine and mail them out. Pretty tacky, huh? You may as well address your letter to "resident." But with word processing software that has the capability to generate form letters, you can have each copy of your announcement addressed and personalized to each party you want to notify. All you need to do is make a list of the names and addresses in a separate word processing document (or you could use a *database* file; we'll discuss the electronic filing system next), and then type up a letter that looked something like this:

```
    October 9, 1986

    «FirstName» «LastName»
    «Address»
    «City»,«State» «Zip»

    Dear «FirstName»;

    We are moving our offices to Century City. We should be all
moved in by October 23rd. So please, change your records to
reflect this. Here is our new address:

                      Hot Stuff Management
                      2222 E. Park West , Suite 1313
                      Century City, CA 90067

    Thank you.
```

If you look closely, you can figure out what's going on. The announcement is set up with "holes" into which new data from the list is successively inserted each time an announcement is printed. The holes are set apart from the regular text by a special symbol (i.e. "«»"). The computer will automatically print as many announcements as there are names on the list.

Now you can use that list again to address all the envelopes. Addressing envelopes can be done by printing right on the envelope or using adhesive labels. In fact, you can even print a label with your new address and include it in your letter so recipients can just stick the label over their old one on their rolodex card. Then again, your recipient may be computerized too, which would mean that *their* rolodex information is all on disk. More on that later.

In any case, this method of sending out announcements, notices, letters, invitations, and other types of correspondence is faster, neater, and better organized than using the manual procedures of yesteryear.

Another practical application for word processing is in the writing up of contracts, confirmations, *riders*, and other documents. Having contract drafts already drawn up and ready for use will make your operation much more efficient. The insertion of specific names, dates, terms, and other items is easy. Then, of course, the negotiations process is also simplified since drafts can be sent back and forth between parties, with appropriate changes to the documents made when necessary. Or, if negotiations are being handled in person, the changes, additions and deletions can be made on the spot, greatly expediting the closing of a deal.

Word processing will also save you time if you do any sort of billing or monthly statements. You can keep your blank invoice and statement forms on disk ready to be filled in. When it comes time to bill, you need only update the new balances and print them out. No more starting from scratch each month.

A lot of people feel uncomfortable about switching to word processing after years of dealing with paper. They don't want to have part of their files on disk and part of their files in the filing cabinet. And they don't want to redo everything just to get it onto word processing disks. It's understandable if you feel that way. Fortunately, there's a solution to this problem that may be practical for you. It's a process called scanning. Using an *optical character reader* (OCR), it's possible to transfer a type-written page directly onto disk without manual typing. OCR scanners are fairly expensive right now (anywhere between $500 and $30,000), but the technology is there, and prices will most certainly drop as manufacturing techniques improve and demand for the product increases. The good news is that you can rent an OCR or hire a service that can do the scanning for you.

It doesn't look too exciting, but this DEST Optical Character Reader (OCR) can save a lot of time and money if you have a tremendous amount of typed information to get onto disk.

Speaking of high-tech, high-priced goodies, how about a laser printer ($2000-$8000) for your office? A laser printer will generate output that looks like it's been professionally typeset. (As a matter of fact, this book was typeset with a laser printer — text as well as graphics.) If you do a lot of flyers or use a graphic design/typesetting service very often, this could be a good investment. Again, if you can't afford a laser printer you can rent time on one at many of the copy shops that are getting into this new technology.

Many music industry professionals see word processing as the single most important function of their automated office, simply because it's so versatile. Like other businesses, the music field is incredibly dependent on written communication. If you're concerned with image and efficiency in your work environment, maybe it's time to put aside the typewriter and explore the enticing world of word processing.

Files At Your Fingertips

All right, we've picked on the old typewriter long enough. Let's move on to the filing cabinet. Keeping files on clients or individuals you deal with is an absolute necessity in this business. Maybe you also need to keep an up-to-date list of radio stations, record companies, recording studios, or sound equipment rental companies. The small computers available today make it possible to maintain a neat and orderly filing system that allows you to do virtually anything you want with the information in the files, and in less time than you could do the same task manually.

Computerized filing or *database managment* is perfect for handling information that needs to be updated frequently. That's why banks, stockbrokers and airlines use computers so much. But before we get into the miracles of having an electronic filing system, let's first dispel some myths about keeping information in a computer.

Myth #1: The information gets into the computer by an act of God. Not true. Keeping a *database* requires data entry, and data entry requires a little patience and consistency on the part of whoever's entering the data. If you don't plan to take the time to keep your database up to date, making a conversion to a computerized method would be a waste of time.

Myth #2: A database will completely eliminate the need for hardcopy (paper) files. Also not true. In some cases, the paper load will even increase because the computer allows you to deal effectively with more information than you were able to handle before.

Myth #3: Computerizing your files means you'll be locked into organizing your files the way the computer program dictates, not the way you want them. On the contrary, most file management *programs* let you set up your files in a way that best suits you and the way you work.

Using an electronic filing system offers three major advantages:

- Organization — There's really no better way to keep files organized. The computer won't let you mess anything up or lose anything. Everything is neat, tidy, and legible. Best of all, you always know where to find things when you need them.
- Data Manipulation — With the assistance of database management software, the computer can search through all your records very fast to find the information you need. But that's not all. It will take that information and do whatever you want with it. Do you need a list? Do you need mailing labels? Do you need the names to be included in a memo or letter? Also, information can be updated easily so that your records are kept current.
- Saved Space — Literally thousands of records can be stored on a single diskette. As a central storage area for your needed information, the disk functions much like a file cabinet, but occupies less space.

Let's look at a classic candidate to put in the electronic filing cabinet. Of course, it's a people file. You know, that rolodex on your desk, or that messy address book you keep full of business cards and pieces of loose paper with numbers on them? Using a computer database to keep track of business and personal contacts lets you organize that information in various ways.

A database works something like this: Each individual unit of information like "first name" or "job description" gets put into sort of an imaginary box called a *field*. One complete set of fields, (e.g. first name, last name, street, city, st, zip, phone etc.) makes up one *record*. A group of records is called a *file*. File management software lets you visually arrange your fields on the computer screen and add little labels to designate what information should go where, so entering information into your database is just like filling out a customized form.

Finding a particular persons record is as easy as giving the computer a value to match. For instance if you wanted to find "Joe Smith's" phone number you would be presented with an empty form. You would then type "Smith" in the last name field. The computer would then check the last name field in all the records until it finds all the matches for "Smith". Quick as wink you would see Joe's complete record on the screen.

This computerized rolodex is a very handy thing, but it's not always efficient to start up your computer just to look up one person's phone number. So don't throw away your rolodex or little black book just yet. The real advantage of an electronic

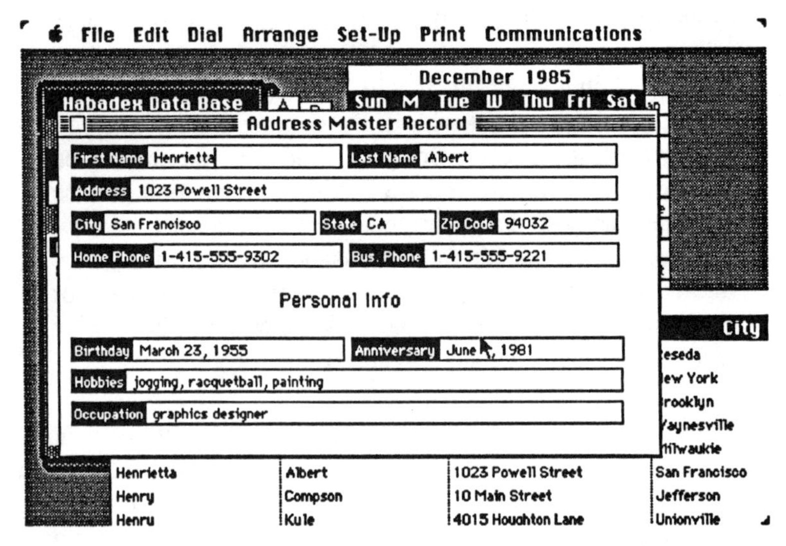

This is a good example of a "people" file using a program called Habadex™ on the Macintosh.

filing system comes into focus when you need to look through a whole file and extract a group or sub-category. For instance, you may only want a list of *A&R* (*Artist and Repertoire*) people in the New York area. Or maybe you just need to know what session players you have on file.

Here's another example. Let's say you have five hundred entries, or records, on file and you have to do a mailing to the press to announce a benefit concert or showcase that you need publicized. If, when you originally entered names into the computer, you included a field that described each person's job title, it will then be easy for you to extract the one hundred and fifty names in your database of journalists, *publicists*, editors, and other press-related people. And once you've extracted these records from the file, you can print out labels, form letters, lists or whatever you need.

When you think about it, there are a lot of occasions when you need a list: a guest list, a list of radio stations, a list of studios, a song list, a check list, a list of lists. Computers are great at compiling lists. Whatever data you have stored on your computer can be output as a list — fast. But there's more to it than just having the ability to sort and list at will. With a computerized filing system, you can easily store miscellaneous information within each record that will help you remember different things about each person. Perhaps you want to include birthday or anniversary information. You can even include notations to yourself or your staff about the people you have on file.

Forms and Labels

Computers with graphics capabilities can make short work of forms and labels needed in the office. Having the ability to make up your own customized forms any time you need to is an extremely useful and convenient luxury. If you need people to get information for you, creating a form they can use will help ensure that the job gets done to your liking. Checklists are another good idea, especially when you're training a new employee or supervising temporary help.

There are literally hundreds of ways you can utilize this form-generation capability. You can create your own job applications, petty cash forms, expense reports, and whatever else you need in order to do your job.

But that's not all. We already talked about mailing labels, but other kinds of labels can be generated on a small computer system as well. One great example would be labels for audio and video tapes. Many people in the music business deal with literally hundreds of tapes. A consistent label format for all the cassette tapes you file or mail out might keep things better organized and make searching for a particular tape a lot easier.

You can organize the cataloging and content of each tape on a computer too, logging names of songs, the performing artists and their affiliations, the writers, copyright data and other pertinent information.

An A&R representative of a record company, for example, can make great use of a tape cataloging system. It can also make life easier for music supervisors and producers who round-up songs for film soundtracks. People in these kind of jobs receive hundreds upon hundreds of cassettes every week. The criteria used to catalog the material will depend on the specific needs of the user. One method might be to breakdown the tapes into music categories, like 'Heavy Metal', 'R & B', or 'Blues.' Or you can create descriptive key words like 'Stones-style R&R' or 'Synth-pop.' This method allows you to instantly get a list of songs that match a requested criteria. The list would also indicate the location of the tape on which the song resides ("Tape #47, Box B"), and where on the tape the song can be found ("side 1, track 3").

Now all you'll have to do is get used to being so damned organized!

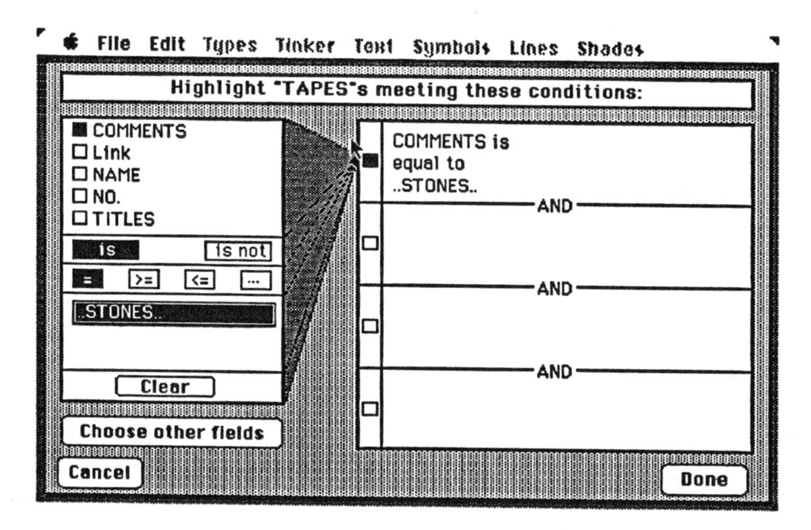

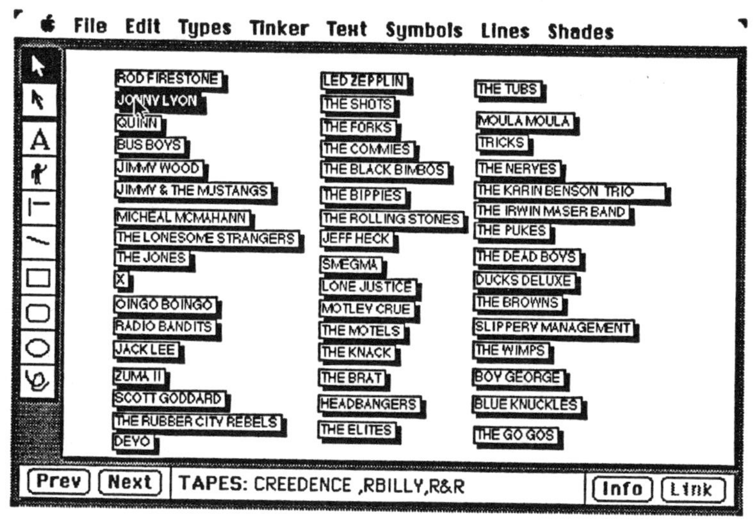

Using a database product called Filevision™, tapes can be catalogued by various criteria.

CONNECTION 1.1

ARTIST MANAGERS

Perhaps one of the toughest jobs in the music industry is managing the career of a performer. *Personal managers* and *business managers* are responsible for the growth and nurturing of an artist's career, and their work requires them to be highly organized and efficient. It makes sense that their need for a computer would be great. Rick London, business manager for singer Billy Joel and famed producer Phil Ramone, uses a computerized system that automates all of his accounting needs including general ledger and cash flow reports. "We generate financial statements for over seventy-five different companies," said London from his New York office. "If I didn't have the computer, I'd have to hire a hell of a lot of bookkeepers."

London believes that the music industry was, at first, somewhat apprehensive about incorporating computers into the normal scheme of things. But he thinks things are beginning to change. "It was kind of like the horse and plow," he said. "All of a sudden someone came out with a tractor that presented a new and better way of getting the job done. The problem was that some people just didn't have the resources to purchase that tractor. Or, perhaps right before the tractor came out, they had gone out and bought a brand new horse and plow."

London's office also uses word processing, electronic mail and a sophisticated software package called Cash Digest, which handles bill paying and income collection for his clients.

On the other coast, in Los Angeles, Jerry Weintraub manages Neil Diamond, but it is Diamond's own company, Arch Angel Productions, that coordinates the singer's activities. According to Barry Cardineal of Arch Angel, the company has for some time been using a Macintosh computer to help out on the road, and is now beginning to take advantage of its organizing abilities for a number of office applications. One area that's particularly in need of computer control is Neil Diamond's extensive tape library.

"When you've been recording for over twenty years," said Cardineal, "you accumulate many, many tapes and they're all stored in different locations. We're aiming for a system that will keep track of exactly what's on each tape and exactly where each tape can be found."

Managers for the groups Foreigner, Tina Turner, Dio and others are using variations of a software package called ARTMAN, which is specifically geared toward the needs of a personal manager. Developed by Fox Productions (see CONNECTION 3.2) and marketed by Mainline Software Inc., both based in Pennsylvania, ARTMAN is one of a series of expertly designed programs, developed solely for use by professionals in the music industry. Managers use ARTMAN to keep track of money, time, and people. The system includes a sophisticated rolodex-style database of the manager's business and personal contacts, a personal calendar, a detailed history file of each artist, a guest list program that facilitates simple and efficient guest list control, ticket count and *settlement* modules, a *merchandising* file to track sales and availabilities of T-Shirts, and many other features and functions. There's even a module that stores details regarding the membership status, contacts and figures of a fan club. In addition Fox Productions provides complete installation, customized program modifications, personalized training, well-written *documentation*, and follow up software maintenance.

Of course, there are many managers out there working with artists who aren't as well known as the Neil Diamonds, Billy Joels and Tina Turners of the world. But even on the lower rungs of the music business, managers are slowly but surely beginning to use affordable computer systems.

P.J. Birosik is president of a company called Ready To Rock, a multi-divisional entertainment company based in Los Angeles. The company handles personal management, production, and music publishing for various heavy metal bands, including Armored Saint and Steeler.

"Speaking as an independent personal manager," said Birosik, "a lot of the computer systems that are used for our kind of business are financially out of reach for most people. You have to remember that most personal managers don't make a lot of money, because most of them don't have signed groups. I would guess that about 80% of the personal managers actively operating in the United States don't have acts signed to major labels. Therefore, they do not have the kind of income to invest in technology such as computers."

Through a timesharing agreement with other tenants in her office building, Birosik is able to computerize what must be the music industry's most tedious task: The Dread Mailing.

"Personal managers are always sending out reams of paper mail," she said, "so when I want to send out a letter to twenty-five hundred radio stations throughout the country about an artist of mine that's coming out with an independent album, I just draft one master letter. My secretary then types the basic form letter into the computer, and it automatically prints a personalized, letter-fresh copy to each each individual I need to send correspondence to."

Birosik keeps master address lists of A&R representatives at record companies, of national journalists, of local journalists and of college and urban radio stations across the country. "This process," says Birosik, "saves me and my secretary a tremendous amount of time."

Birosik recalls how life was before the computer, when a mass mailing meant running off a thousand copies of an original letter and then manually typing in a name and address on each copy. "Imagine a slightly graying, middle aged manager rapidly getting older because it's about a quarter to 2, and she's crouched over a typewriter, frantically trying to make the 8 a.m. mail. We used to have to work until the wee hours of the morning trying to hand-crank out these letters." She admits it was a cost savings, but says, "It didn't look very personalized. In fact, it looked pretty sleazy."

Like other managers who are already incorporating computers into their work, Birosik would like to see more of her peers in the industry using telecommunication systems in their offices (see CONNECTION 2.1). "We all go through a very manual process when we need someone else to review the text of a contract, a bio or a recording studio arrangement. There's always a two or three day delay waiting for mail to arrive and trying to connect on the telephone. If more people used electronic mail,

complete messages would be delivered immediately along with the material to be reviewed. The revisions could then be sent back on the computer as soon as they were done. To get things done fast, it's an absolute necessity."

CONNECTION 1.2

THE RECORD COMPANIES

In the heart of Hollywood stands one of the most unusual office buildings known to man. The Capitol Records Tower is a large, white cylindrical structure that looks more like a reject from a nearby studio back lot than the oversized stack of record disks it is purported to simulate. The company that had this structure built in 1957 was among the first of the large record companies to incorporate computers into its business, having implemented a *mainframe* system in the late sixties. Today, however, Captiol Records is struggling to break free of its dependence on a large centralized computer system and move toward the flexibility and efficiency available on small desktop *microcomputers*.

All of America's major record companies have been moving significantly more slowly into office technology than have other large corporations. One reason might be that the record industry has always been regarded as a "people industry" (Why invest in cold computers that take up a lot of room and are only good at crunching numbers?) The arrival of personal computers that are, in a sense, "people computers" has changed all that. They are small, they can do almost anything you want them to do and, best of all, you don't have to know much about computers to use them.

Capitol, for example, is still tied to their mainframe computer system, but many departments within the organization are beginning to bring personal computers into their work. Personal computers (*IBM PC's*) are being used for budget and financial analysis, sales tracking, forecasting, royalty and licensing applications, investment analysis and deal negotiation analysis (See CONNECTION 4.2).

Capitol is determined to push even further into the personal computer arena. The Management Information Services (*MIS*) department is in the process of incorporating word processing systems into various departments throughout the organization. So far, three departments — legal, business affairs and MIS — are using word processing, and the publicity and A&R departments are next.

Richard Ulaszek, head of the MIS department, said that one of Capitol's priorities is to make it possible for personal computers to extract, or download, information from the large mainframe. Once the information is downloaded, it can be manipulated and examined on personal computers, which are much easier to use than the giant corporate computer systems.

"There's a lot of nice things that you can do on a personal computer, that you can't do on a mainframe," said Ulaszek. "Eventually, personal computers and the mainframe will work with each other very easily and there won't be a wide gap between using one and using the other, the way there is right now. As time goes on and as technology changes, I think the two will be merged. On the other hand, there's a lot of heavyweight tasks that you can do on the mainframe that would swamp a personal computer. The problem is that we haven't found an efficient and inexpensive way to make that link yet. One software item we were considering was not that good, in my opinion, yet it was priced at about $125,000 plus $800 per machine. We're not talking peanuts here."

Other record companies, including Warner Bros. and Motown, are already downloading data from their mainframes to their personal computer systems. Warner Bros. Records, one of the record companies furthest along in computerized office automation, uses personal computers extensively in almost every department including legal, publicity, promotion, finance, administration, payroll, and personnel. The company also has telecommunications capability between its corporate offices in New York, Nashville, and Burbank and between manufacturing plants (where records are pressed).

Besides having the ability to share data between personal computers and a large computer, Motown Record Company makes good use of computerized databases, particularly in the promotional and publicity areas. But, unlike Capitol and Warner Bros., Motown runs its royalty and accounting systems exclusively on their mainframe.

As you might expect, the smaller, albeit younger, record companies are jumping into microcomputer systems at a steady rate. I.R.S. Records, an independent label under MCA Records' powerful distribution arm, uses custom-written software, which runs on their IBM PC, to simplify the complex tracking of royalty payments to their artists. Rhino Records, a successful independent label specializing in novelty records and videos, now uses word processing for writing up contracts and correspondence. Rhino is also looking into other computer systems, including the Macintosh, to help out in the art department and in its growing mail-order business.

CONNECTION 1.3

THE MUSIC PUBLISHERS

The administrative procedures for song publishing and artist/writer royalty payments are complex, requiring a lot of specialized calculations and a massive amount of paper work. Not surprisingly, computers have played an important role in music publishing for years now. ASCAP and BMI, the two largest performing rights organizations in the world, have tremendously sophisticated computer systems. In Europe, performing rights societies are allowing *publishers* to notify them, via computer telecommunications, concerning the acquisition of new song material. This means that a publisher can enter the data into its own system, which is set up to notify the society automatically.

Bob Katovsky, a computer *consultant* based in England, has installed computer systems for many large music companies around the world. According to Katovsky, the newest trend for the large publishing houses is to have personal computers hooked up to large mainframe systems so that employees can still perform the usual range of personal computing functions such as *spreadsheet* modeling and graphics. "The type of systems that are being developed," said Katovsky, "are not just to keep track of dollars and cents for the accountants. I installed one professional system that monitors who the song has been offered to and the response. This copyright monitoring system allows a publisher to keep track of every song it controls. This could be 200 songs or 200,000."

MCA Records has probably one of the most sophisticated copyright and publishing systems in the business. The system allows anyone in the company to get all the information they need off the computer. "You can scan for information based on whatever you happen to know," said Joan Monnery of MCA. "Before we had the computer system, we had an index card for the title of each song on each album, a card for each artist, and a card for each album. This was a tremendous amount of paperwork and it was very difficult to update everything. Now, let's say somebody wants to find a song written by an artist named Dan Hartman, and they don't know that he had a song called "Dream About You" on the "Streets Of Fire" soundtrack album. All they have to do is enter "Dan Hartman" and all the information will come up on the screen. The same information will come up if they enter in the title of the song or the title of the album. Everything you'd want to know about each song is on the system including the recording date, the composer, the publisher, the release date, the royalty rate, the producer, the arranger and the date we entered the information into the computer."

Like other applications in the music industry, publishing and royalty accounting is not limited to the big companies with the big budgets. The same type of work can be accomplished on small scale *hardware* and software for a fraction of the cost that the big firms are paying for their systems.

As personal manager for guitarist Robin Trower and others, Derek Sutton applies his industry know-how to his own spreadsheet software and is able to keep close tabs on his artists' royalty earnings. "Artists generally have the wrong impression about how much money they can make from records," Sutton said. "The money that a band is going to make from records is always considerably less than what they think they're going to make, so I use a spreadsheet model to show them exactly what's going on. If, for example, there's a shared writing arrangement among five or six members, the income will not be spread evenly throughout the band. So if I want to know what everybody makes, I have to have a way of splitting out what the income is by the proportions of writing that they do. A spreadsheet software package allows me to do that."

Also using a personal computer is Michael O'Connor, an independent publisher who has represented recorded material for Roger Miller, Crystal Gayle, Glen Campbell, Johnny Mathis, Kenny Rogers, Karen Carpenter and others. "I've basically been a one-man operation for many years," said O'Connor, "and without the computer it would have been impossible. My computer is like an army of secretaries for me."

O'Connor believes his personal computer system is superior to the publishing and royalty accounting systems of the large record companies. "Your standard programmer does not understand the intricacies of the music business, and they're the ones designing these systems for the large record companies. The large corporations are being advised by systems analysts who want to sell big programs. One record company has a program that creates mailing lists, and it cost them $20,000. They don't realize that they can get that same program for about $300. With the use of database and word processing software on a personal computer, a major company can save thousands upon thousands of dollars on their publishing systems. But the systems analysts don't want to recommend the cheapest way to go. They want to recommend the way that will make them the most money. It's an inherent conflict of interest."

Using his IBM PC, O'Connor is able to generate high quality letters to people at all the record companies in order to pitch his material. "If I had to do that manually," he said, "it would take a week to get all the mail out for one song. My computer can do it in about a half hour, and that includes the printing of labels for the tape cassettes. The other thing I do is the royalty accounting. The software does the addition and the subtraction, and by virtue of it being a database, it can print out reports sorted by song, by writer, by country, or by any other indicator that I want."

Now that he's so automated, we asked O'Connor if he can imagine running his business today without the use of computers. "No, I can't imagine it," he said. "I would either get out of the music business altogether or look for a cliff to jump off of."

Chapter Two

STAYING IN TOUCH

Having discussed computerized filing systems and how keeping a people database can simplify your work life, let's take that concept one step further and talk about how a computer can help keep your office functions (and you!) better organized. In this chapter, we'll talk about telecommunications, electronic mail, and automated scheduling.

Hanging On The Telephone

One way to use an electronic filing system for telephone convenience is in compiling a list of all the people (and phone numbers) you plan to call in a given day. You (or an assistant or secretary) can just go down the list, checking off names as you make your calls. You can also keep the computer running on your desk, bringing up people's records on the screen while you talk to them on the phone. This can help if you need to refresh your memory about a particular caller. You can also jot down any notes and enter them in the record as soon as the call is over.

Besides enabling you to take notes and store them right there in a particular record, some database programs have a built-in memory dialer capability. You indicate the name of the person or company, the computer finds the number in your database and, through a special hook-up with the phone, dials the number for you.

One version of this type of program even keeps a phone log that tracks who you called, how long you talked and how much money the phone company charged you for the call. This logging capability really comes in handy, especially if you charge or get charged by the hour. It's also a fantastic way to ensure accurate tracking for expenses and tax deductions. You can even specify a time or dollar limit on a particular call so that the computer will automatically let you know when you've reached your self-imposed limit.

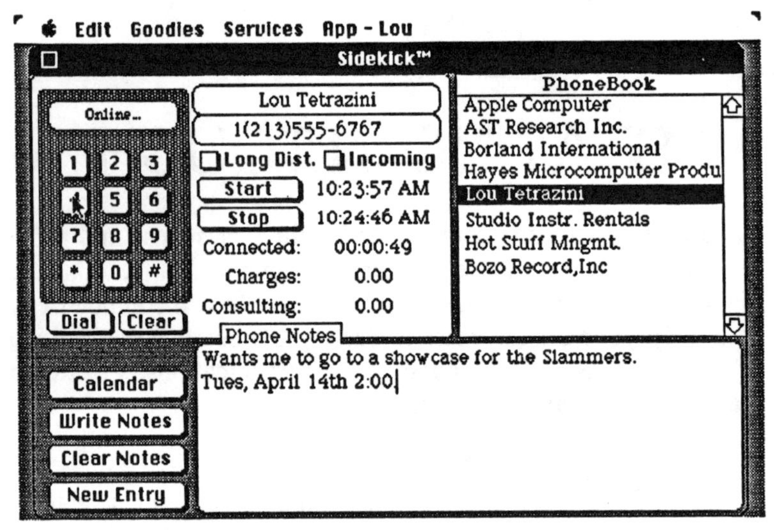

Sidekick™ software works along with a Macintosh to make it easier then ever to reach out and touch someone.

As technology marches forward, telephones and computer hardware are becoming more and more integrated. Now that AT&T is selling personal computers, it's likely we'll see computers that combine the functions of a telephone and a computer into one unit. There are add-ons now available that work with your computer and telephone to act like a super answering machine. This new innovation is called "voice mail" or "voice messaging". Not only can people leave messages, but they can pick up messages left for their ears only. The way it works is you would give certain people a code to punch in on a touchtone telephone when they call your number. Recognizing their code, the computer would play back any messages left especially for them. This feature allows one computer to function as a personal answering service for several individuals. Incoming and outgoing messages are recorded *digitally* and stored on a *disk*, making this a much more efficient and flexible answering device than the tape machines most of us are using. You can even program the device to call a specified number of people automatically and leave them (or their answering machines) a digitally recorded message. You can be out of the office meeting somebody for lunch while your computer is making calls for you.

While normal voice communication is being enhanced, computer-to-computer communication, or *networking*, is fast becoming a business necessity. Any data your computer can generate (letters, *spreadsheets*, press releases, *itineraries*, etc.) can be sent over the telephone lines to another computer that's equipped to receive. This means that our dependence on the post office and commercial mail carriers may well diminish in the near future as the use of computer telecommunications (often referred to as *electronic mail* or *E-mail*) becomes more prevalent throughout the music industry.

Is electronic mail better than a phone? Well, that depends on how you're using it (See CONNECTIONS 2.1 and 5.5). If you need to contact someone who lives in the same city you do, it probably makes more sense to just use the phone. But when you need to contact someone overseas, to be in touch with people who are on the road or just hard to reach by phone, E-mail is just the ticket. It also comes in handy if you need to get documents, lists, or some other kind of written detail to someone.

The requirements for using E-mail are that you subscribe to one of the networks and that you have a computer, a *modem* and *telecommunications software*. It is also helpful if the other party is similarly equipped. As an example, here's a list of some major features of the IMC E-Mail system (See CONNECTION 5.5), one of the more popular communication networks in the music industry (other networks have similar features, some provide more, some less):

- •Instantaneous delivery — Messages and documents can be sent around the world, any day of the week (even holidays).
- •Multiple copies — It's almost as easy to send a letter or memo to twenty people as to one. All you need to do is give the computer one letter and a list of names.
- •Courtesy copies, blind copies — Just type CC or BC along with the appropriate names.
- •Forwarding — If you want to pass on a letter you've received to someone else, you just type F and the name(s).
- •Automatic receipt — As soon as someone reads your letter, a receipt is sent back to you automatically as a mail item. In other words, you always know if (and when) the message you sent out was read by the person you sent it to.
- •Automated reply — After you've read a mail item you've received, you can just type R and your reply message. The computer will know who to send the reply back to. It's also possible to attach the original letter to your reply for reference. You just type AP.
- •Date activated — This capability allows you to send a letter today but specify that you don't want it delivered until a specified date in the future (great for birthdays!). You can also specify a certain time. This device can be used to send yourself reminders, too.
- •Spelling checker — This checks the spelling on your outgoing correspondence for you.

- Files your mail — All incoming and outgoing mail is kept on file in the system until you delete it. You can search your mail by name, subject, a word, a phrase or date.
- Send telex and mailgrams — You can send mail to someone without a computer, because IMC's E-mail gives you access to the U.S. Postal Service, E-Com, MCI-Mail, Western Union's EasyLink, and other services.

A new feature called *voice mail*, now available on AT&T's electronic mail system, allows you the option of getting your E-mail without the use of a computer. Messages are read to you over the phone by the system's computer, which uses a sophisticated voice synthesis technique.

At present, E-mail is not replacing the telephone in the office, but it is becoming an important communications tool that is making better communicators out of a lot of people in the music business. The way things stand now, networks like IMC are "closed circuits" in which communication takes place primarily between subscribers. But in the future communication among the various networks should be possible.

When Can We Do Lunch?

So now your pal the computer can find a number, dial the phone, answer the phone, keep a log, track your charges, send and receive mail, and serve as an all around, convenient desktop organizer. But there's more. Right along with all these nifty features, you also get time management.

Any office environment needs a calendar to keep track of appointments, dates, gigs, and other things to remember. The computer can provide you with an automated method of staying on top of your busy schedule and you can even set things up so your system will remind you of important appointments coming up.

Many of the personal computers now available come equipped with a battery-powered, built-in calendar/clock. This means they know the date and time of day whenever they're switched on. If you mark on your computerized calendar that you have a meeting on March 5th at 3:00 p.m., come the 5th, a calendar program will remind you of your appointments that day. The system allows you to enter "things to do", birthdays, and anything else you would put onto a desk or wall calendar. These programs are set up very much like the popular Day-at-a-Glance, Week-at-a-Glance, Month-at-a-Glance books you see at the stationery store. The difference is that the calendar is on your computer, all neat and orderly. One of the by-products of all this is that it gives you an organized record of everything you did all year. This enables you to easily reconstruct your schedule for tax purposes, or for a questioning client, with just a single keystroke.

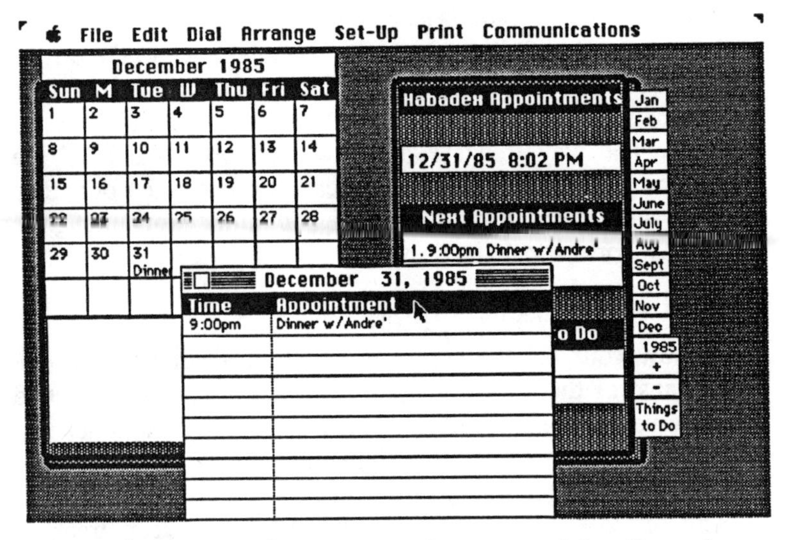

Habadex™ helps to keep your appointments straight, all year long.

CONNECTION 2.1

TELECOMMUNICATIONS IN THE OFFICE

The music industry is about five years ahead of most other industries in its use of telecommunications. It's not just separate firms that are using computers to conference between their own offices. It's more like two thousand different companies and individuals worldwide who are talking to each other on-line.The technology of telecommunications seems custom made for the touring segment of the music business (See CONNECTION 5.5). And now more and more music professionals working in offices are following suit.

Laura Annick is executive director of the Wheatley Organization, a southern California management firm that represents the Little River Band, Real Life, and FX, as well as other bands from Australia, the United States and Europe. "Electronic mail is basically our means of communication with the groups we handle overseas," said Annick. "We can actually do day-to-day business as if they were right here in the same city. With the time difference in Australia, it's 9:00 in the morning there when it's 4:00 in the afternoon our time, a day ahead. So it really can set us back and delay projects. But by using computer telecommunications, we can keep working at a capacity that we wouldn't be able to do if we had to do everything over the telephone."

One band the Wheatley Organization represents, Real Life, recorded an album in Berlin. At the same time, the artwork for the album was being produced in London, and other group-related activity was taking place in both Australia and the United States. "Without this communication," Annick said, "we certainly would not be able to handle all this international involvement. We're currently considering representing a band in Germany, and the entire contract is being negotiated over E-mail. If we weren't using it, the phone calls alone would have been just about as much as our legal fees."

London-based computer consultant, Bob Katovsky has been helping to install computer systems for over nine years for companies like Warner Bros., EMI, Chrysalis, and other major music firms on both continents. "I was introduced to E-mail in

1982," said Katovsky, "and at that time I knew of it but had not really used it myself. The moment I began using it, I became a true convert. I immediately saw the practicalities of it and also how I could cut the cost of long distance communications. The main problem with E–mail is that a lot of people use it as a novelty rather than using it the way it was meant to be used. I don't think that it replaces telephones, but it sure does make the telex and the postal systems obsolete. I believe that, in time, everyone will have an electronic mail box, just as they have a telephone number."

Sharon Weisz, owner of W3 Public Relations, a Los Angeles firm that has represented Deep Purple, Dio, and others, was skeptical at first about whether she would have any use for the electronic mail service she signed up for with International Management Communications (IMC), the music industry's leading telecommunications network. "I really had no idea the system would become so important," said Weisz, "but about six months after getting the computer, we realized we would be working with a band that was coming over from Australia. We were dealing with them three months before they ever got to the States, and I knew the phone calls back and forth were going to be very expensive. It made so much more sense to communicate with them by E-mail. Because of E-mail, there's a definite difference between the way we used to do things and the way we are capable of doing things now. It's pretty amazing."

CONNECTION 2.2

THE DESKTOP CONCEPT

A new development in software for personal computers is called the "desktop metaphor". The idea behind this concept in software is to imitate real life and real office objects in order to let people do things in ways that are more familiar to them. For instance, when you look to see what files are stored on a disk, instead of a list of names, you may see what looks like a file folder on the screen. Some software programs may go so far as to show a file cabinet with differently labeled drawers. Inside the drawers would be folders and inside the folders would be the individual files, represented as sheets of paper with dog-eared corners.

File folders are just one small example of the *desktop metaphor.* New products strive to integrate many different office appliances and give you access on what is called an "interrupt basis". This is the way we all work in real life. For example, when you're drafting a letter and the phone rings, you don't

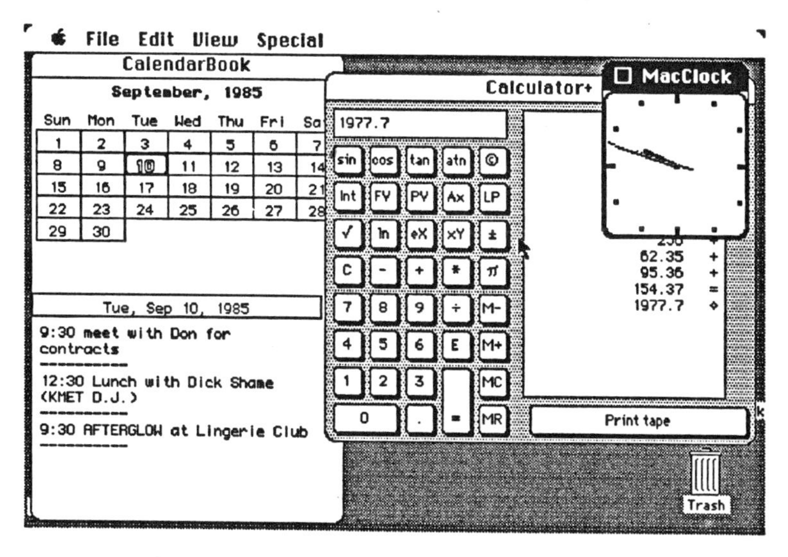

Sidekick™, used with the Macintosh, is a classic example of desktop software.

put your paper and pencil away and clean off your desk just to answer the phone. You interrupt what you're doing (you stop writing) and then you answer the phone. While you're on the phone, you take notes; then when the call is complete, you return to your letter-writing. New software and hardware products for the office computer allow you to put certain operations in the background while you run another program in the foreground. It's just like switching from function to function, just as you would move from the rolodex to the file cabinet.

The *Macintosh*, *Amiga*, *Atari ST*, and newer software environments for the *IBM PC* (such as GEM, Microsoft Windows, and Topview), offer such desktop metaphors as calculators, notepads, rolodex, alarm clocks and appointment books, to name a few. Programs that incorporate the desktop metaphor make the transition to computers a cinch, since the electronic versions look and behave similarly to the real thing. Because your learning time is reduced, you can get right to business.

Chapter Three

TRACKING THE CASH

Most people in our industry don't care much for bookkeeping. That's probably one reason why most of us are doing something in music instead of working for Prudential. Nevertheless, the day may come when the question "Where does all the money go?" must be answered.

In the past, getting the answer usually meant doing hours of manual calculations yourself, or hiring an accountant and then waiting forever for an appointment so that you could get a detailed, costly, and potentially confusing report on your finances. Sometimes, by the time you received the report, the status of your accounts had already changed.

A computer in the organization immediately changes the flow of current information, making it possible for you to get a good, solid answer to that nagging question. Once you sit down and learn how to use one of the many accounting software programs, you'll have, at your fingertips, all the financial information you'll need to make key business decisions, as well as the ammunition to calm the nerves of clients, partners, investors, colleagues, and even an occasional IRS representative.

The new computer technology makes it possible for you to keep your finances in reasonably good shape without requiring that you be an expert in general ledger accounting or computers. Computers handle numbers like it was their lifeblood, and in a way, it is. It's almost impossible for the computer to make an arithmetic error (knock on silicon). So, as long as you feed your system the right numbers, you don't have to worry about the accuracy of the calculations. A computer will speed up everything you do while keeping your books current, accurate and secure.

Using a computer to keep your books makes it easier to keep everybody in your organization well informed. Keeping your books on a computer gives you the ability to print out a report in minutes, whenever the need arises. You can have balance sheets, profit and loss statements, income statements, disbursements, cash flow analysis, graphs, and budgets. It's almost like having your own in-house accounting department.

Many accounting programs also produce excellent historical records that will come in handy when tax time rolls around, when you apply for credit, or if you're ever audited.

There are basically three different categories of software that can be used for keeping your finances in order: specialized accounting software for the music industry, off-the-shelf small business accounting packages, and off-the-shelf database and spreadsheet programs.

Specialized Accounting Software For The Music Industry

First, there are all-in-one packages specifically designed for the music industry. Packages of this sort can include accounting as one part of a multi-function program. One company that designs software specifically for the music industry is Fox Productions, (see CONNECTION 3.2). Fox has developed a line of software for promoters, talent agents, artist managers, facility managers, and other industry pros. These products are designed as full service office management tools that include filing and scheduling capabilities, as well as accounting functions.

Off-the-Shelf Small Business Accounting Packages

Programs that are written specifically to address the needs of the music business provide many built-in conveniences, but you pay a price for these custom capabilities — anywhere from $500-$10,000. Fortunately, there are less expensive alternatives: off-the-shelf small business accounting packages. These products are generic, in that they are designed for use by any type of small business, be it a butcher, a baker or a personal manager for a Japanese James Brown impersonator. In fact, there are lots of off-the-shelf accounting programs designed for small business use that will work fine within the context of the music industry.

All of the accounting principles are built right into the programs, so there's no need to be a bookkeeping expert. Basically, all you have to do is follow the directions and study the examples provided in the printed instruction manuals (often referred to as *documentation*). The software lets you set up "journals" that look very similar to the way hand-written journals might look. You set up a *chart of accounts* where each account will be one of five types: asset, liability, income, expense or checking. You can maintain a number of different checking or savings accounts and get reports on one of your accounts, all of your accounts, or any combination thereof. It may sound like a difficult thing for someone with no bookkeeping or computer experience, but it's really not.

One thing that makes using an accounting software package so simple is that even though the programs employ the *double-entry bookkeeping* technique, transactions need only be entered into the computer once. All affected accounts are updated automatically. Once you've set up your accounts, it's virtually as easy as posting checks. If you have a series of payments that must be made on a regular basis, the whole process can be automated so that with just a few keystrokes a whole set of weekly or monthly transactions are entered into the record. And, if you choose, the checks can be printed on a printer. (For more on simple accounting programs see CONNECTION 3.1 which describes Dollars and Sense, a fine example of an easy to use small business accounting program).

Off-the-Shelf Database and Spreadsheet Programs

The third software alternative for keeping books and daily records is to use off-the-shelf database management and spreadsheet programs. This is more of a do-it-yourself approach, but in some cases, it can provide even more flexibility than the small business accounting programs.

A database or file manager program can do a great job of recording all your expenses. By using the report and sort features of these programs, you can get a list of all the checks written last week, last year or whenever. The search features will let you request a list of checks written to a particular party. The report you generate might include the date the check was

File Edit Formula Format Data Options Macro Window

N59

CHECK REGISTER:1

	A	B	C	D	E	F	G
1	NO.	DATE	DISCRIPTION	CAT	√	AMOUNT	BALANC
2			BEGINNING BALANCE				13,000.(
3	100	3/7/85	JIM BRADLEY	CREW		(250.00)	12,750.(
4	101	3/9/85	DAVE	CREW		(250.00)	12,500.(
5	102	3/11/85	SIR	EQUIP		(350.00)	12,150.(
6	DEP	3/13/85	CAPITAIN RECORDS	REC		7,534.00	19,684.(
7	104	3/15/85	LOU TETRAZINI	COMM		(1,506.80)	18,177.2
8	105	3/17/85	GEM STUDIOS	RCRD		(2,500.00)	15,677.2
9	DEP	3/17/85	THE BONE CLUB	PERF		2,500.00	18,177.2
10	106	3/19/85	MEDIA CONNE			)	15,601.2
11	107	3/21/85	GUITAR LAND			)	14,851.2
12	108	3/23/85	LET IT ROCK			)	14,772.5
13							
14							
15							
16							
17							

CHECK REGISTER:2

Expense Totals	
Crew	500.00
Recording	7,534.00
Equipment	1,100.00
Costumes	78.67

A check register/cash disbursement journal can be easily created with a spreadheet program like Excel™.

written, the check number, the amount, and maybe even a reminder or comment that was made at the time the check was written. Another report can be run to list checks sorted according to their expense category (advertising, recording, promotion, incidentals, etc.). You can also instruct a database management program to provide subtotals for each expense category and give you a handy breakdown of where your money is going.

Using off-the-shelf software is probably the most cost-efficient method of tracking your finances. With a spread-sheet program, for example, you can create your own general ledger, cash disbursements journal, or check register. You're going to have to take the time, however, to create the proper worksheet, and this means being familiar enough with the program (and a few basic accounting principles) to do this. You may want to bypass this step and have a "template" made for you by someone who has done it before. A template is a pre-designed worksheet with all the columns and formulas already in place. Or, you can purchase templates from various vendors.

CONNECTION 3.1

DOLLARS & SENSE

To get an idea of what financial management by computer is all about, let's look at one program called Dollars & Sense. Versions of this program will run on a variety of Apple and IBM compatible personal computers. Dollars & Sense is not the most comprehensive accounting program you can buy, but it is fairly simple to learn and costs less than $175. In most cases, it is quite adequate for in-house bookkeeping tasks.

The first thing you need to do in order to start using Dollars & Sense is to set up a chart of accounts. A chart of accounts will define categories for all your income and expenses. The program supplies you with some pre-designed charts of accounts which you can start with and modify to suit your own needs. You must place each of your accounts into a category that describes its type. Your choices are: assets, liabilities, income, expenses, and checking accounts.

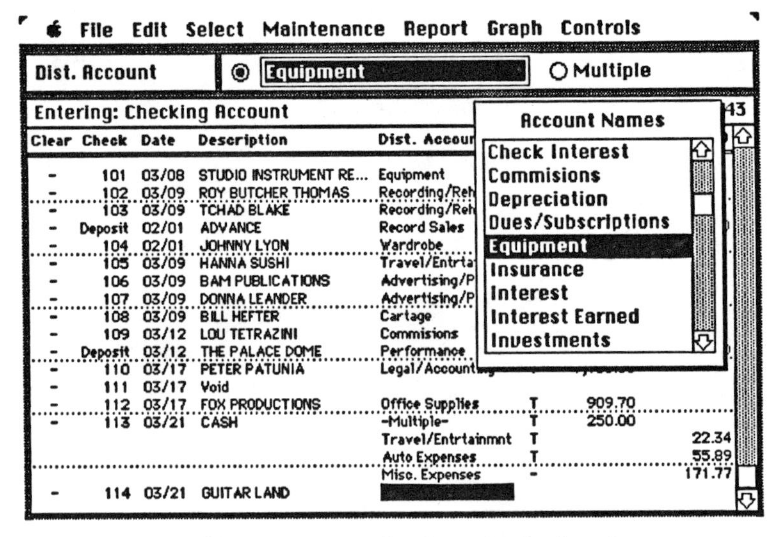

Double entry accounting is made simple using Dollars & Sense™.

As you define each account, the program gives you the option of assigning a monthly budget amount. For example, if you had a monthly rent payment of $231 for a rehearsal space, that would be your budget amount for that account. However, if you had a quarterly payment for insurance, you would enter that amount in just the months that you make those particular payments (January, April, July, October). The program will average them out over twelve months to give you a monthly budget. The program will let you assign budgets to income accounts as well.

When you're finished defining your accounts, you end up with a net annual budget amount, which is derived from all your monthly budgets. If this number is negative, then you know you're running in the red. This feature lets you see the effects of changes in your cash flow and what effect a change in cash flow will have on your bottom line. For instance, you could set up a temporary account just to see the effects of leasing an equipment van. You may find out you can do it, but you can't spend more than $200 a month.

Once you've set up your chart of accounts, you can start entering transactions. Mainly, this means posting checks and allocating them to accounts. You enter the usual information: number, date, description and amount, just as you would enter in your checkbook. But the program also needs to know to which account each expense or deposit should be posted.

Since the program uses the double-entry bookkeeping method, each transaction will affect at least two accounts. A debit to one (the checking account) will credit another (an expense account). To make this happen, you just type the account name, or select it from a list that you can display on the screen. Using a name (i.e."rent") is a lot easier than having to remember the standard numeric account codes (i.e."10009"). Single entries can be posted to multiple accounts, such as in the case of a bank loan, where some of the payment goes to principal and the rest to interest (which is tax deductible).

You only have to post the information once. The computer does all the calculations and automatically updates all other affected accounts. Cash transactions, deposits, and transfers are all handled in this way. And while you're posting, Dollars & Sense is showing you a running balance.

Not only is Dollars & Sense a great way to keep records, it can also help you budget and plan for the future. Before you write a check, you can type in a few hypothetical checks and see what happens to your balances. You'll see the results instantly, and if you can't afford to spend the money, you just change the amounts or erase the entry. No harm done.

This program can also make short work of reconciling your monthly bank statement and can even print checks on the printer. If you have a series of checks that need to be written every month, such as a payroll or regular bills, this may save you a lot of time. By the way, the program developers are now in the process of devising a way to get Dollars & Sense to work in conjunction with many of the electronic banking services being offered. This direct hook-up between your computer and the banks' computers promises to speed things up considerably.

Probably the most useful feature of Dollars & Sense (or any accounting program) is its reporting capability. Dollars & Sense has a very flexible reporting system that will print out balance sheets, income statements, cash flow analysis, and a "monthly budget vs. actual totals" report, to name a few. You can get a list of all your transactions or specify transactions with regard to dates, payees, amounts, or any criteria you choose. For example, you may want a list of every check written to a particular studio between April 1 and July 9. Not only can Dollars & Sense report to you in words and numbers, it will also produce a whole series of graphs based on account information you specify.

Dollars & Sense is one of many simple accounting programs available. It is marketed as a home product as opposed to a full-blown business package. Depending on your situation, you may need a more sophisticated accounting package written specifically for small business. A business package will be a little harder to work with and will certainly cost more, but most of the advantages and underlying principles will resemble what we've described here for Dollars & Sense.

CONNECTION 3.2

FINANCES WITH FOX PRODUCTIONS

Fox Productions designs business management software packages specifically intended for use by artist managers, tour accountants, booking and talent agencies, concert promoters, music industry merchandisers, equipment rental houses, as well as by managers of civic centers, arenas, and concert halls. Heading Fox Productions is David Cooper, who comes from a family of musicians and was heavily involved in the booking and promoting of student rock concerts during his college days. Cooper is also a virtual whiz-kid in accounting with an incredible understanding of its practical applications to the music industry.

All of Cooper's software packages use a general ledger that functions as a cash receipt/cash disbursement system. "Out of all the different accounting methods," said Cooper, "this is the only one that will work in the music business. It's a cash business."

According to Cooper, the journal entry system is "idiot-proof," and merely requires the user to provide the computer with answers to five simple questions about the transaction. "When you enter a date, a company code, where the money is going to or being disbursed from, a description of the disbursement or receipt and an amount, the system will produce reports that will tell you everything you need to know about your business."

The output generated by the Fox accounting systems includes an income statement, a trial balance summary, a trial balance detail, a journal reference report, an account master summary, and a transaction date report. "It's really a financial controlling system," said Cooper, "because you can look back at any account and see what was charged to that account, what was budgeted, and what the variance is between the actual and projected amounts."

All the Fox systems use a multi-company general ledger. "This means you can define many companies inside your office, and then charge things to different accounts in your chart of accounts. The different company codes are simply a logical grouping of accounts. In a rental equipment package, for example, instead of calling them different companies, they might separate their accounts by packs. If there were, say, various pieces of equipment that the group Foreigner had, each piece would be attached to a company code called the Foreigner Pack. The same holds true in a promoter's office, but promoters are more worried about advertising or production costs. If you're a promoter writing a check to radio station WKRP for six different events that they advertised in the last month, you can charge specific dollar amounts out of the total check amount to the separate events."

John Bauer Concerts/Media One, a concert promoter based in Seattle, that purchased Fox Productions' promoter system (FOXPRO) in 1983. The company uses FOXPRO primarily for office accounting and the tracking of building availabilities and advertising. Before the purchase of FOXPRO, someone had to write out all of the company's accounting information by hand and send it to an outside bookkeeping service. Now, instead of waiting weeks for business summaries, the company gets instant reports, both actual and projected, any time they're needed.

According to Bauer executive assistant Debbie Ward, their FOXPRO system generates a series of reports on command and can calculate break even points for possible future concerts based on information entered on a specific show. "Our method also does building availabilities," said Ward. "This means that at any time, I can go on the system and find out if a venue is available on a particular date. We only call the buildings once a week to update our records, so we're not spending the time on the phone that we used to."

This type of friendly, custom-made software does not come cheap. A typical system from Fox Productions can cost anywhere between $5000 and $7000. This cost usually includes installation, training, documentation, and customer support.

"We did a lot of serious shopping to try and find a computer that would fulfill our needs," said Ward. "But we were unable to use most of the systems we looked at because the programs did not understand the special needs of our business. When we do a show, we figure out how much we made or lost, and that's it. We just go on to the next show. There's no accounts payable, which makes our business unique. When David Cooper showed us his programs, I knew that we had finally found somebody who really understood what a computer had to be able to do for us."

Chapter Four

PLANNING IT OUT

Admittedly, the music business is full of surprises. Your big break (or ruination) can come from out of the blue. Predicting how things will go is more art than science. More luck than logic. But despite the oddities of this crazy business, your chances for success on any level are much greater when you put some thought and planning into your endeavors. If you want to make a record, you're better off knowing how much time and money it will cost all together, rather than moving along, step by step, unaware of whether or not you'll be able to make it to the next phase. Of course we're not just talking about records here. We're talking about any project you set out to do — be it a tour, a video, a publicity campaign, or the start of a new business within the industry. The point is that if you plan carefully, you have a better shot at reaching your goal.

In this chapter, we'll discuss how personal computers can be used as a tool for planning.

The Budget

Sooner or later, everybody in the industry has to create a budget for one thing or another. There's no getting around it. Unless you have unlimited funds to work with (dream on), a well thought out budget is an absolute must for anything that will cost you (or someone else) time and money.

Even if you don't particularly like working with numbers, you'll probably find that creating a budget on a small computer with spreadsheet software is easy, fast, and accurate and that the result is more useful than any budget you've ever done by hand. Quite simply, spreadsheet software has done for budgeting what word processing has done for writing.

There are three big reasons why budgets and spreadsheets are perfect for each other. First, all the calculations are done by the computer and there's almost no chance of any arithmetic errors creeping in as long as you've input the correct numbers. Second, as always on a computer, your work will be neat, tidy, and organized, with no crossed out or erased numbers. There's no more need to have a budget retyped so you can mail or present it to someone else. When you're ready to print it out, it will be in presentation-quality condition. Third, a computerized budget offers the luxury of saying "What If..?" and getting an answer in seconds. In other words, a spreadsheet allows you to experiment with different numbers and scenarios and see the results instantly without tiresome recalculations. Now that's good planning!

Most spreadsheet programs, like Lotus 1-2-3, Multiplan, and Excel allow you to create models, or worksheets, in order to formulate your budgets. These models are like blank forms with all your columns and headings set up, similar to a tax form. You need only go down the form and fill in the blank cells with your numbers. The computer will do all the calculations for you. If you decide to change a particular number on the page, the computer, on command, will recalculate, giving you your new totals.

Let's suppose you were using an electronic spreadsheet to put together a recording budget. You might look down at the bottom line and say "Ouch!" So now you want to see if cutting back to double scale (studio musicians, union pay scale) instead of triple scale will make a difference. Or, what if you decided on a $35 an hour studio for over-dubs instead of the more expensive one you had hoped to use. The spreadsheet will recalculate your budget every time you make a change.

The entire process of putting out an independent record release can be thoroughly planned and budgeted (see CONNECTION 4.3), from recording, to pressing, to marketing. Putting together a concise budget can give you good ammunition to use when hunting down a backer and, at the very least, help you keep costs (and your anxiety about getting in over your head) under control.

Another good use for a spreadsheet program is in the concert promotion game, where there is a very detailed method for costing out shows. A spreadsheet model can be set up to aid the promoter in *scaling the house* (determining various ticket prices), figuring his breakeven point, *gross potential*, percentages,

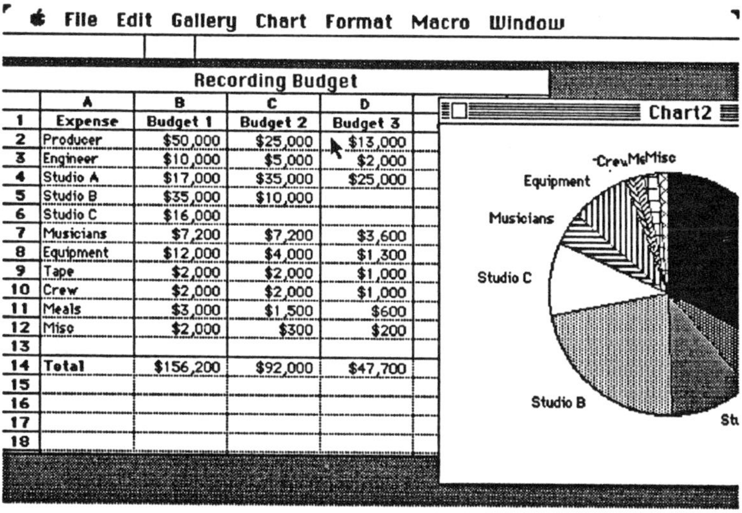

File Edit Gallery Chart Format Macro Window

Recording Budget

	A	B	C	D
1	Expense	Budget 1	Budget 2	Budget 3
2	Producer	$50,000	$25,000	$13,000
3	Engineer	$10,000	$5,000	$2,000
4	Studio A	$17,000	$35,000	$25,000
5	Studio B	$35,000	$10,000	
6	Studio C	$16,000		
7	Musicians	$7,200	$7,200	$3,600
8	Equipment	$12,000	$4,000	$1,300
9	Tape	$2,000	$2,000	$1,000
10	Crew	$2,000	$2,000	$1,000
11	Meals	$3,000	$1,500	$600
12	Misc	$2,000	$300	$200
13				
14	Total	$156,200	$92,000	$47,700
15				
16				
17				
18				

Chart2

Crew Meals Misc
Equipment
Musicians
Studio C
Studio B

Spreadsheet software, such as Excel™, can do wonders when it comes to working up budgets for recording and other projects.

expenses, advertising cost and amusement taxes. A promoter who had a computer doing the calculations would be in a position to put in a realistic bid for an act while he still has the booking agent on the phone. (For more on promoters, see Connection 5.4).

Spreadsheets can be set up and used over and over for different projects, cutting down the time it takes to do a detailed, realistic budget to less than an hour. Budgets can be set up so that you can enter not only the projected cost of each line item, but also the actual cost, once the money has been spent. You can easily create a variance column that will let you know at a glance how far off your cost predictions were from the actual amounts. You'll see where you have estimated too high or too low and will be able to apply that knowledge to the next budget you build.

Through The Past, Darkly

Keeping budgets, both actual and projected, on the computer gives you a good source of information to go back to when you're planning your next project. Without racking your brain, trying to remember approximately what it cost you last year to do something, you can simply review previous budgets and see exactly. This approach applies not only to budgets, but to all the information that is compiled and stored on your computer. A database containing details of past tours (see CONNECTION 4.1), recording sessions, video productions, promotional campaigns, and other activities can provide valuable information that you can recycle during the planning stages of future projects. There's no need to dig out old files in dusty drawers or make a bunch of phone calls to find the information you need from years gone by. All you have to do is pull out a disk and bring up the information you need onto the computer screen.

Gathering Information

Let's face it, you need to accumulate accurate information to make good decisions about your project. A computer, gives you a variety of ways to do just that. Besides storing budgets and historical files, a personal computer can serve as a centralized information appliance, allowing you to gather information more efficiently than ever.

Through the wonder of telecommunications, your computer can provide a cost-effective way to get detailed information, sometimes instantly, from across town or across continents. Various information networks you can subscribe to, such as CompuServe, International Management Communications (IMC), Instant Access and the Performing Artists Network (PAN) provide access to all kinds of information. For example, if you subscribe to IMC, you can read *on-line* brochures and resumes from many of the top support services in the industry (i.e. tour management, production services, sound, lights, studios, etc.). You can also make inquiries via electronic mail to these services and can even get bids and job estimates in a matter of hours instead of days or weeks. The correspondence you receive from these services is virtually the same as having received a written response. Unlike a phone conversation, which has the potential for mis-communication, the electronic mail process leaves both parties with a complete record of what was discussed.

You can also connect with huge on-line data banks that contain such useful information as domestic and international airline flights, hotel/motel accommodations, restaurants, exchange rates, customs restrictions, weather, international law and a whole lot more. More specific to the music industry, there are on-line information services that specialize in up to the minute information needed by concert promoters, agents, and music groups. This data includes facility specs, *itineraries*, and specifics on the touring acts.

Getting The Big Picture

A lot of planning needs to be done before a budget can even be started. What are the time parameters? What markets are important? What resources are needed and which ones are available? Not only are these factors interdependent, but the order in which they are executed can be critical to the success or failure of the overall project. With the use of *flowcharts* and timeline charts, you can begin to see how a project consists of many separate tasks, many of which are interconnected. Certain tasks must be completed before others can begin. If these tasks don't end on schedule, other task deadlines, (sometimes called "milestones"), will be affected, as will the project deadline itself. By getting the big picture of a project in this way, you're able to discern immediately what has to be done when, and in what order.

When you're planning a large-scale project, such as a tour or the making of an album (see CONNECTION 4.3) or video, it sometimes helps to get an overview of all the steps that are necessary to reach your final goal. A computer equipped with a project management or planning program can help you "chart" a project from start to finish, giving you a concise and easy-to-understand picture of your work process.

Project management programs are designed to handle the three most important items on everybody's agenda: time, people, and money. When programs of this type first came out, they were capable of handling only one project at a time. Some of the newer releases are designed for one project or several.

Various other kinds of software can also be used to gain a broad perspective of a situation during the planning stages. Spreadsheet models are often used by record labels, managers and artists for deal analysis when they're planning to sit down to negotiate a contract (see CONNECTION 4.2). This is done by creating a spreadsheet model that will show what potential a record or publishing deal has to offer for each party involved. What will 7 points gross the artist if he sells 300,000 units? What is the effect of 10% *freegoods* when sales are over one million? What is the break-even sales point? Using a computer for this type of planning can show you what a contract is really worth before it's too late to make changes.

CONNECTION 4.1

PLANNING A TOUR

A touring organization has to have a budget, an itinerary and a schedule to follow. Derek Sutton, manager of rock guitarist Robin Trower and other artists based in both Europe and America, admitted that before he started using computers, planning a tour was all guesswork and trial and error decisions. "I was always hazarding guesses and flying by the seat of my pants," said Sutton, who also managed the seventies super-group Styx during their heyday. "Now I have spreadsheet models for all kinds of tours, be they club dates with very few people, or massive tours using seven semis and a large number of people in various categories of expense. Using these models, I can estimate very, very closely what the expenses are going to be. Because I have built the models, I can plug in a bunch of numbers for just about anybody, and have a forecast within hours of being given certain parameters."

Sutton uses his portable computer system for virtually every facet of his business, but he takes special pride in the planning and budgeting advantages it gives him. "I can show a client in England that if they come to the states and do a six week tour, they can go home with approximately X amount of dollars in their pocket. Whereas if they come in for four weeks, they will go home having made nothing. With the computer, I can show them exactly where all the money is going. They can then tell me that they're going to double up in the hotel rooms, and I can punch a couple buttons (hit a couple keys) and show them that it won't be saving them as much as they think. It's just a matter of being able to say 'Look, this is what happens. This is how the costs effect *your* bottom line.'"

Sutton believes that the advent of spreadsheet programs like VisiCalc and Multiplan is what put personal computers on the map in the first place. "For me," he said, "trying to convince somebody that it's either possible or not to do a tour, a spreadsheet is an absolute necessity. To do it the other way would mean investing vast amounts of time slaving over numbers and doing recalculations. It's now become less of an art and more of a real business. I don't know how I ever worked without it before."

The economic realities of the eighties have made the use of a computer for tour planning an invaluable tool for Sutton, especially when consulting with his clients. "Some artists get into a particular mode of thinking when it comes to touring," he said. "A few years back, an artist may have been at the top end of the scale, touring arenas, using limousines, traveling first class or chartered flights. But when an artist is no longer at that level, I can lay out a set of figures and say, 'This is the way you can do it. You can fly first class and the tour will cost you $50,000. You can go coach class and you'll just about break even. Or, you can travel on the ground in a motor home and you'll go home with $25,000 in your pocket.' Then, I can ask them straight out, 'Are you going on tour to make a living, or are you going on tour to fluff your own ego?'"

A perfect case in point is when Sutton advised one of his clients on the affordability of doing a cross-country North American tour. "Before I had used spreadsheet models," said Sutton, "I would have immediately said that a tour would be unprofitable for him. But because I can show him exactly what has to be done in order to make a profit, he is now making money on the road. That is something he hasn't done for over a dozen years."

To aid the touring industry as a whole in the planning of road tours, *Performance* magazine has recently initiated an on-line database called the Instant Access System, which provides subscribers with up-to-date information that can be accessed using a computer and modem. The system includes information on touring companies in all major cities, scheduled shows, scheduled acts, box office histories, details on facilities and promoters, listings of talent agencies and their rosters, and practically anything else that a production manager or tour manager might need to know to better plan a tour.

Computer consultant Janet Ritz, whose clients include Bill Graham Presents, Winterland Productions, Huey Lewis and the News, Howard Jones, and CBS Records, recently assisted tour manager John Toomey in the planning of George Thorogood's cross-country U.S. tour. "I highly recommend the PFS family

GRUPO INCOGNITO
TOUR EXPENSES AND INCOME
1985 TOUR

TOTAL TOUR EXPENSE
##################

	ACTUAL	BUDGETED
OVERHEAD	7247.13	7300.00
SALARIES	17150.00	16450.00
PAYROLL TAXES	3430.00	3290.00
W.COMP INS	1029.00	987.00
TRAVEL/HOTELS	50950.30	53161.25
PER DIEM	10025.00	8750.00
MISCELLANEOUS	6938.86	7800.00
==================================		
TOTAL	96770.29	97738.25

TOUR INCOME		174430.00
AGENCY COMMISSION	10	17443.00
EXPENSES		96770.29
		++++++++++
SURPLUS		60216.71
		++++++++++
US MGT COMMISION	.2	12043.00
DUE TO GRUPO INCOGNITO		48173.71
LESS COST AND CASH ADVANCED		31400.47
HELD FOR IRS (30%)		14452.11
TOTAL PAYABLE		2321.13

##############################

USE BUDGETED OR ACTUAL? 0/1 1

OVERHEAD

	BUDGETED RATE/DY/W	#PERIODS	AMOUNT	ACTUAL
REHEARSAL	500	1	500.00	621.00
MONITORS	50	2	100.00	
INSTRMTS	50	2	100.00	
CARTAGE	100	3	300.00	150.00
RFRSHMTS	50	2	100.00	91.88
IMMIGRATION	2000	1	2000.00	2712.75
INSURANCE		0	4200.00	3250.00
STOLEN FROM ROAD MANAGER				421.50
======================				
SUB-TOTAL			7300.00	7247.13

CREW

POSITION	NAME	SALARY	#PRDS	AMOUNT	
TOUR MGR	toni	600	7	4200.00	4200.00
DRUMS/SOUND	tim	550	8	4400.00	4700.00
GUITS/LIGHTS	steve	500	8	4000.00	4150.00
MONITORS	allan	550	7	3850.00	4100.00
======================					
SUB-TOTAL				16450.00	17150.00

Here's an example of a spreadsheet model used to budget a tour. (Notice the budgeted and actual column.)

of software for road managers," said Ritz. "It's very user friendly and it allows you to design your own files any way you want. For the Thorogood tour, John constructed a massive database, with all of his venue information. It included anything he would possibly have to call on. He set up about 25 different forms including form letters, guest list forms, hotel rooming list forms, and other things that he needs at every venue he goes to. When he gets to each venue, he just types in the name of the city, and the program searches through the database, and starts spitting out the forms he needs on his printer. It's really incredible. What he used to do was get to a venue and spend a good six or seven hours filling out these forms. Now, it's just a matter of typing one word and pushing a button."

There are contracts, riders, confirmations, specifications, inquiries, and a lot of other correspondence to be generated when planning a tour. It's always best to get things in writing and a computer makes it easier to do so. Greg Kihn's *road manager*, Pat Caples, also uses a computer for tour planning and preparation. "All of our advance work is done on our system," said Caples. "Our production manager uses a database system and a word processor, and I never have to see anything on paper until the actual tour begins."

Caples says that storing historical data has really helped out in the planning of a tour. "We can recall any piece of information we want. Let's say that a year and half from now we'll want to know about the last gig we did in Houston. We'll be able to go back to search for that show and we immediately see what the attendance was, what the gross was, and all the other pertinent information. Since we design our own forms, we can put a little space for comments that can help us when we're retrieving information. For example, we can indicate that the lighting company we used wasn't very enthusiastic, or whatever. We can keep that information and it's easy to recall, without taking up a lot of space."

Greg Kihn's organization uses a few different types of computers including the Apple IIc and the Macintosh. "I love our computers," admitted Caples. "There's just so many things you can keep in your head, and there's no way you can remember it all. You have to have somewhere to store all that information and still be able to get back to it."

```
<< 03/12/85 >>        ! SHOW   ! B'MINGHAM ! CIVIC CTR !

  VENUE:BIRMINGHAM CIVIC CENTAR              PHONE:      205-328-8160
        1 CIVIC CENTER PLAZXA                PRODUCTION:205-323-6127
        BIRMINGHAM, ALABAMA  35203
        CASEY JONES (MGR)

  PROMOTER:TONY RUFFINO                      PHONE:(205)979-4352
  CONTACT: MIKE TRUCKS/GARY WEINBERGER       PHONE:

  RIGGING TIME:8 AM      MAIN CALL:10 AM    # 2 CALL:NO

  DOORS AT:6:00                            SWOW AT:      8:00
  CAPACITY:19,000                          TYPE SEATING: GA

  MILES IN:254                             MILES OUT:    246
         CREW                                              BAND
BIRMINGHAM HYATT                     HOTEL          SAME
901 21ST STREET                     ADDRESS 1
                                    ADDRESS 2
BIRMINGHAM, ALAABAMA  35203      CITY,STATE,ZIP
(205)322-1234                        PHONE
(CR)calendar (f1)hardcopy (f2)previous (f3)next (f4)menu (f10)exp 2 (C)


<< 03/12/85 >>        ! SHOW   ! B'MINGHAM ! CIVIC CTR !
  RIGGING CALL:8 AM     STAGE HANDS:3U/2D    LOADERS:4/I FRK   RIGGERS:
  MAIN CALL    :10 AM   STAGE HANDS:10       LOADERS:2ND FRK   PUSHERS:
  # 2 CALL     :NO      STAGE HANDS:         LOADERS:          PUSHERS:
  SHOW CALL    :NO      STAGE HANDS:         LOADERS:          SPOT OP:
  OUT CALL     :NO      STAGE HANDS:         LOADERS:          PUSHERS:
  RIG OUT      :NO      STAGE HANDS:         LOADERS:          PUSHERS:

  CATERING:                                 PHONE:
   RIG CALL TIME :7:30      HOW MANY:15         MENU: PASTRIES/BEVERAGES
   BREAKFAST TIME:9 AM      HOW MANY:30+UNION   MENU: AS PER RIDER
   LUNCH TIME    :1PM       HOW MANY:55+UNION   MENU: DELI DEATH
   DINNER TIME   :NO        HOW MANY:           MENU: MEATLOAF/EGGPLANT
   POST SHOW TIME:NO        HOW MANY:           MENU:
   BAND DRESSING ROOM HOT FOOD:TBA

  DRESS & TUNE HOW MANY:              DISTANCE:
  POWER:              HEAT:             AIR COND:                SHOWERS:

  COMMENTS:VIDEO


(CR)calendar (f1)hardcopy (f2)previous (f3)next (f4)menu (f10)exp 3 (C)
```

A history report like this provides all the important data on a particular venue.

CONNECTION 4.2

SUCH A DEAL?

The ultimate dream for thousands of struggling musicians is getting that signed contract with a record company — any record company. But like other contracts in other types of businesses, the agreement between artist and label is anything but standard. Each contract is unique and designed specifically for the two parties involved. The details of each contract are usually hammered out in a series of meetings between label and artist representatives. Today, many record companies are using personal computers to review, calculate and experiment with the fine details of a recording contract in order to be better prepared for negotiations. In the music business, this is referred to as deal analysis.

Standard variables of a recording contract that are unique to each individual artist — advances, artist *royalties*, video commitments, publishing royalties, cooperative advertising, etc. — are all entered into the system. An analyst can then play with the numbers to see how certain changes effect the total agreement and determine what direction the negotiations should go.

At Capitol Records, it's the people in the business affairs department who are involved in the actual contract negotiations with the artists. But the information they use to negotiate comes out of the financial analysis department where the deals are now analyzed using IBM PCs. Pat Rothwell, who has been with Capitol for twenty-three years, is the manager of the department. According to Rothwell, deal analysis was initially done on Capitol's mainframe computer system, but her department has recently started using the IBM PCs with very good results. "The record industry is always coming up with new ways to negotiate," said Rothwell, "and it's a rather complex thing to do. There's always so many modifications during contract negotiations, and the PCs are flexible enough to handle all those changes. We often do our analysis in the midst of the negotiations, and the computer is wonderful because it makes it so easy to do that."

Because Captiol has been doing deal analysis for a number of years, the business affairs people have a very good idea about what the company can afford to pay a brand new artist. "For a new act," Rothwell said, "we can immediately show them how many units (records) they need to sell in order to break even. So that kind of deal is more or less set already, except for a few things that might be unique for that particular contract. But where the deal analysis system really starts to work for us is when an artist has been with another label, or if they were with us, and they don't like their current contract. This happens a lot in the music industry, because you cannot compel someone to be creative. And if an artist becomes very successful, and feels that their deal doesn't suit them anymore, we will get into renegotiations."

Sometimes negotiations can last for six months, with as many as ten or fifteen versions of the contract drawn up before an agreement is met. "Having the PC is great," said Rothwell, "because quite often business affairs will come to us for guidance because they just talked to someone's manager on the phone who's coming in tomorrow to discuss a contract. Being able to respond quickly is very important if we're going to be helpful to the people who are negotiating."

Deal analysis on a personal computer doesn't have to be limited to the record companies. Artist managers and entertainment attorneys can also find it useful to review the parameters and fine points of contracts on their personal computers. Derek Sutton, manager of guitarist Robin Trower and others, uses spreadsheet models on his computer to analyze proposed record deals. "I'm able to input all the variable factors into these models," said Sutton, "including the percentage rate of royalty, the producer's royalty rate, the selling price of the album, the selling price of cassette tapes, how the band draws from the royalty account, how many writers there are in the band and everything else that goes into a basic recording contract. The bottom line of my model shows how much each guy in the band will earn for a specified number of album sales."

CONNECTION 4.3

PLANNING AN INDEPENDENT RECORD RELEASE

Releasing a record on your own independent label can be a pretty big job. If you want to do it right, the one thing that can make a big difference is the planning. Marketing considerations may dictate that the record be released at a certain time of year. (You want to make sure your "School's Out" record doesn't arrive in the stores in September and your "Shakin' Christmas" album doesn't come out in January.) When a group effort is required, being able to present a clear-cut plan to the parties involved can make for a more productive team. Having a plan and a means of presenting it can also impress potential backers. And, taking the time to plan out your record project will aid you in setting priorities and goals.

Project management techniques have been developed and used by big corporations and government agencies for years to help in planning and monitoring complex projects. *Critical Path Method (CPM), Program Evaluation and Review Technique (PERT),* and *Gantt* are three of the more popular methods. Only recently have programs that utilize these techniques been available to users of small computers. The upshot of this is that these techniques can be applied to almost any kind of project, big or small. And since the techniques are now built into inexpensive and easy to use programs, you don't have to be a graduate of Harvard Business School to take advantage of them.

MacProject is one such project management program for the Macintosh computer. With MacProject, you manage the three things it takes to get any job done: time, money, and resources. The program allows you to create a flowchart on the screen. If you break your project down into a sequence of tasks, and give each a duration, fixed costs, and a list of resources you plan to use, the program can then calculate earliest start, earliest finish, lead time, lag time, and even cash flow. Once you create the flowchart (see illustration), the program automatically creates five other useful charts, from the information you entered, about each task.

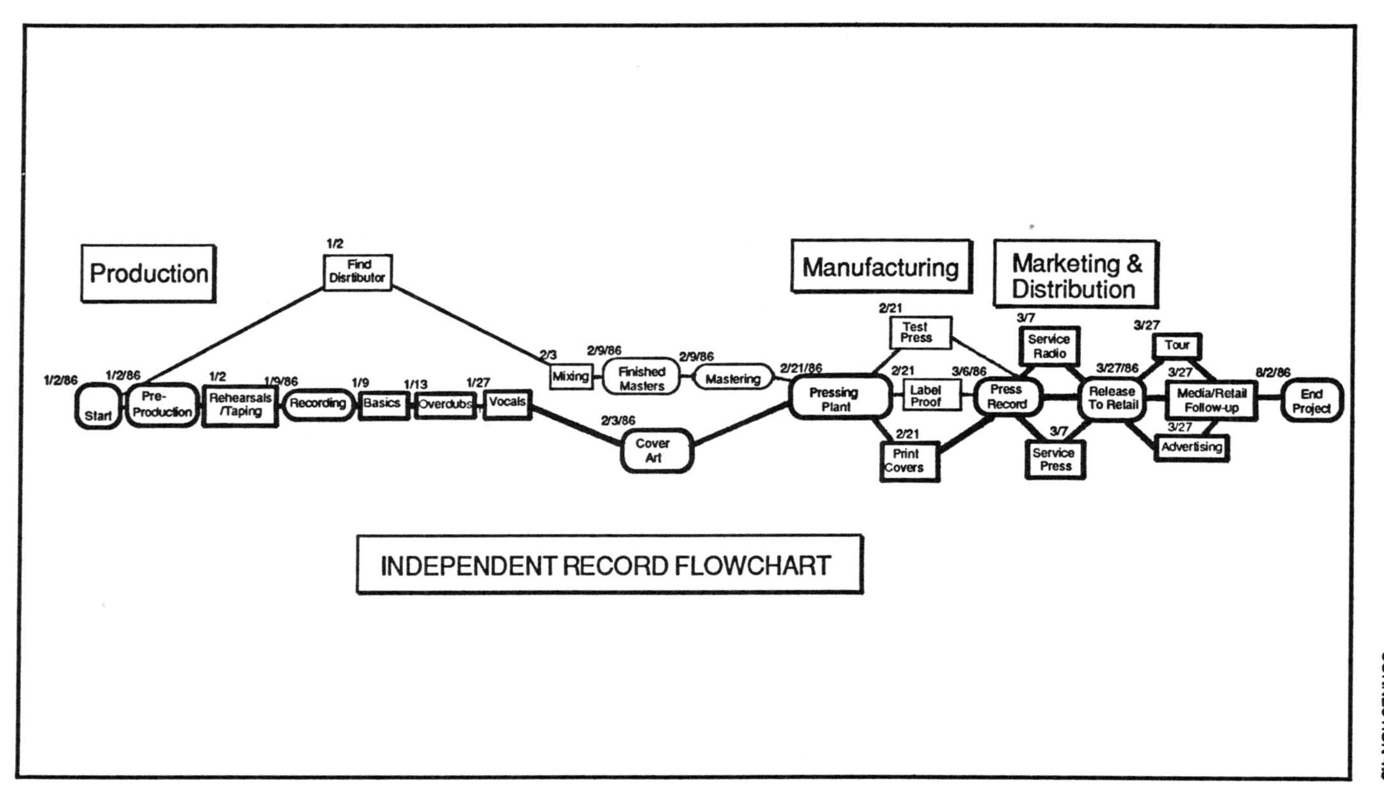
Production
Manufacturing
Marketing & Distribution
1/2/86
Start
1/2/86
Pre-Production
1/2
Find Disrtibutor
1/2
Rehearsals /Taping
1/9/86
Recording
1/9
Basics
1/13
Overdubs
1/27
Vocals
2/3
Mixing
2/9/86
Finished Masters
2/9/86
Mastering
2/3/86
Cover Art
2/21/86
Pressing Plant
2/21
Test Press
2/21
Label Proof
2/21
Print Covers
3/6/86
Press Record
3/7
Service Radio
3/7
Service Press
3/27/86
Release To Retail
3/27
Tour
3/27
Media/Retail Follow-up
3/27
Advertising
8/2/86
End Project
INDEPENDENT RECORD FLOWCHART

The flowchart you see here represents graphically what's involved in getting a record to market. It demonstrates the interaction and dependencies among the intermediate tasks. Milestones, the most important events in a project, are shown as rounded boxes. This chart points out a number of important issues that should be considered in planning an album project.

The flowchart shows that a search for a distributor is begun at (and continued through) the pre-production and recording phase of the project. The logic here is that without a distributor for the product, it might be foolhardy to go into the manufacturing phase.

Producing album graphics can take as long as the audio production. The album jackets should be printed and delivered to the pressing plant before the records are pressed. This is shown by the critical path of the flowchart. Macproject shows the critical path of the project as the path with bolder, darker lines connecting the tasks. Any task along the critical path must be completed on schedule or the project's completion date will fall behind accordingly. Tasks not on the critical path, such as mixing down have a certain amount of slack time, or margin; that is, they may be started a little late or take a few days longer without affecting the completion date.

Sending out promotional copies to radio and the media should be done well in advance of a general release. Radio needs time to listen to all the product they receive and the press has anywhere between a two week and three month lead time on record reviews. If there is some radio action, or some reviews are already happening, it's likely the stores will stock more product. A product that has neither will have a slim chance of being reordered by the stores.

The life of an independent release is many times longer than that of a major label release. There is actually no time limit for an indie from the release date until there is some sort of significant action. Therefore, you should usually give an indie record six months to a year before you write it off.

MacProject will take into consideration which days of the week you want to work, (i.e. Sundays and holidays) and how many hours a day (up to 24) in order to calculate the end date. You can even tell the program what date you want to finish and it will work backward and tell you what date you would need to start. Like a spreadsheet, a project management program lets you change your figures around and ask "what if ?" questions. The program will instantly recalculate the effects of the change on the critical path and indicate the revised project dates.

MacProject is just one of the many pieces of project management software that can do this type of project planning. There's also Superproject, Microsoft Project and Harvard Total Project Manager. Most of these programs are available for use on a variety of personal computers.

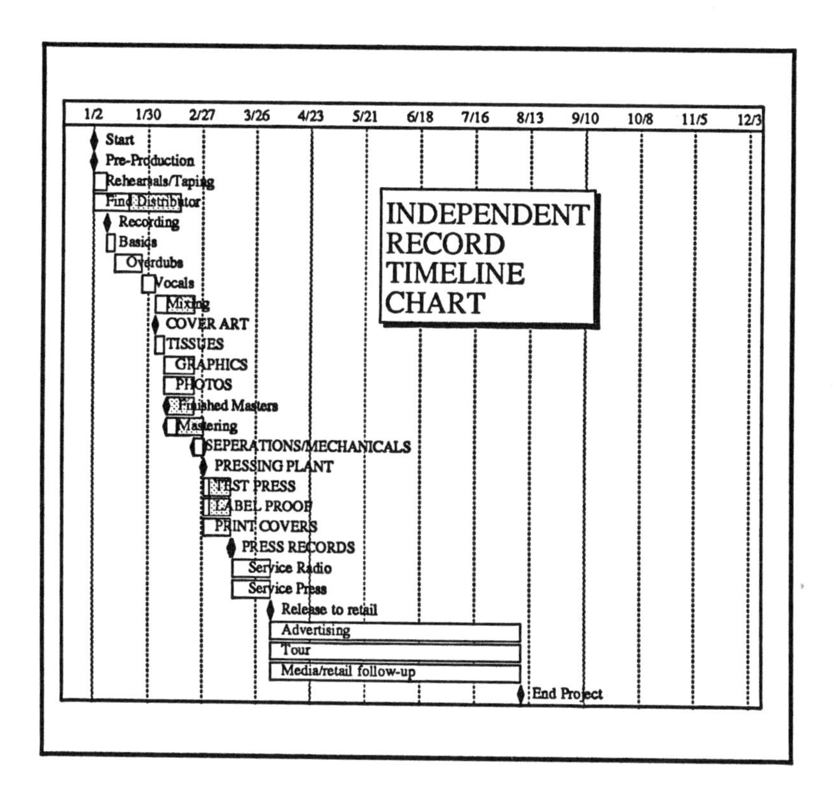

MacProject™, a project management program, can create timeline charts to help manage your time and resources.

Chapter Five

HITTING THE ROAD

A computer on the road with a traveling musical entourage is as commonplace today as a stack of Marshall amplifiers and an electric guitar. Prince, Madonna, U2, Huey Lewis, Tina Turner, Bruce Springsteen, John Cougar Mellenchamp, Rick Springfield, Sting, Lionel Richie, Duran Duran, The Kinks, The Dead, The Stones, Foreigner. No matter who's on tour, you can be sure that the *artist's manager* and *business manager* are most concerned with what has become the single most important item accompanying the band: the personal computer.

Computers are used for tour planning and budgeting, settling up the night's receipts, logging expenses, preparing *itineraries*, doing payroll, making cash flow projections, and handling stage and equipment management. Even communication between the tour's principle organizers is done via computer. We'll cover all

Reporting Date: 01/31/85

Page: 02

KILLER ROCKERS
SETTLEMENT REPORT

EXPENSE DISTRIBUTION

ACCOUNT	BUDGET AMOUNT	BOX OFFICE PAYOUT	PROMOTERS PAYOUT 1	PROMOTERS PAYOUT 2	T O T A L
ACT 2	$1,000.0	$1,000.0	$.0	$.0	$1,000.00
SOUND & LIGHTS	$6,000.0	$6,000.0	$.0	$.0	$6,000.00
ADVERTISING	$4,000.0	$.0	$4,000.0	$.0	$4,000.00
RENT	$7,500.0	$.0	$7,500.0	$.0	$7,500.00
USEAGE TAX	$475.0	$.0	$475.0	$.0	$475.00
INSURANCE	$250.0	$.0	$250.0	$.0	$250.00
BOX OFFICE	$250.0	$.0	$250.0	$.0	$250.00
TICKET PRINTING	$295.0	$.0	$295.0	$.0	$295.00
USHERS/DOORMAN	$300.0	$300.0	$.0	$.0	$300.00
TICKET TAKERS	$100.0	$100.0	$.0	$.0	$100.00
POLICE	$1,000.0	$1,000.0	$.0	$.0	$1,000.00
PRIVATE SECURITY	$2,500.0	$2,500.0	$.0	$.0	$2,500.00
T-SHIRT SECURITY	$250.0	$250.0	$.0	$.0	$250.00
STAGEHANDS	$3,000.0	$3,000.0	$.0	$.0	$3,000.00
LOADERS/RIGGERS	$3,000.0	$3,000.0	$.0	$.0	$3,000.00
ELECTRICIAN	$250.0	$250.0	$.0	$.0	$250.00
STAGE	$2,500.0	$2,500.0	$.0	$.0	$2,500.00
SPOTLIGHTS	$600.0	$600.0	$.0	$.0	$600.00
FORK LIFT	$1,000.0	$1,000.0	$.0	$.0	$1,000.00
DAMAGE	$500.0	$.0	$500.0	$.0	$500.00
ASCAP/BMI	$300.0	$300.0	$.0	$.0	$300.00
CATERING	$1,000.0	$1,000.0	$.0	$.0	$1,000.00
KEYBOARDS/TUNIUNG	$35.0	$35.0	$.0	$.0	$35.00
RUNNER	$25.0	$25.0	$.0	$.0	$25.00
MISC 1 HOUSE STAFF	$1,500.0	$1,500.0	$.0	$.0	$1,500.00
T O T A L S ========>	$37,630.0	$24,360.0	$13,270.0	$.0	$37,630.00

SETTLEMENT SUMMARY

GROSS :	$173,500.00	ARTIST PROFIT :	$114,469.18
TAXES PAID :	$850.00	PROMOTER PROFIT :	$20,550.82
ADJUSTED GROSS :	$172,650.00	PRODUCTION REIMBURSE:	$6,000.00
TOTAL EXPENSES :	$37,630.00	OTHER 1 :	$.00
		OTHER 2 :	$.00
SHOW NET ======>	$135,020.00	TO BE PAID =========>	$120,469.18

COMMENTS on DISPURSION

[ARTIST'S DEAL:$30000]
[GUARANTEE + 85% NET]
[OVER $99375 B=$84469]

Deposit to Agency :	$15,000.00
Cash to Road Manager :	$4,000.00
OTHER 1 :	$.00
OTHER 2 :	$.00
OTHER 3 :	$.00
NET CHECK RECEIVED =====>	$101,469.18

ARTIST'S PERCENTAGE : 66.00 %
PROMOTER PERCENTAGE: 12.00 %
EXPENSES PERCENTAGE : 22.00 %

A typical settlement report generated by FoxPro™, a multi-faceted computer program used in concert promotion.

these areas and more in this chapter, and you'll soon see how computers, over the last couple of years, have become indispensable when the big acts hit the road.

For smaller scale tours, or for bands that want to tour but don't have the vast resources of, say, a Springsteen organization, there's a lot to learn from the way the big boys use their computer systems. In fact, the technology in small, personal computers is so sophisticated (and yet, relatively inexpensive) that many concepts and applications seen on major tours can be scaled down for use in more modest touring situations.

That Settles It!

When the opening act is about to finish, it's time for representatives of the headlining act to meet with the promoter and get paid. In the biz, this is known as the *settlement.* The *gate* and the concession stands have to be counted up, deductions must be taken out, and percentages, breakpoints, bonuses, and taxes must be calculated. For the major league rock and roll stars, settlements can be pretty complicated affairs.

All this used to be a pretty nerve-racking job, but nowadays a computer-packing *road manager* or *tour accountant* (see CONNECTION 5.2) can do it all in a fraction of the time it used to take.

Often, a portable computer is set up right in the production office of the venue and all the necessary calculations such as breakeven, artist's percentage, promoters percentage, and taxes are done with the computer's help.

Systems are now under development that will enable the group's management and the promoter (see CONNECTION 5.4) to share information electronically. When these systems become available, they'll streamline the settlement procedure even further.

Expenses and Payroll

While out on the road, it's tough to carry enough cash to pay a weekly salary and/or *per diem.* Passing out checks while everybody's away from home is pointless anyway, so what is usually done is that the tour accountant or road manager keeps a running account on each individual and when the tour is over, each person gets paid on the basis of the number of days and number of shows worked. But on a typical tour, people need to be paid or advanced something from time to time so that they have some spending money. You never know what might come up. Someone might get sick and need money for medicine, or, if the group is traveling by bus, there might be repair expenses that have to be paid in cash. Who knows? Someone might even need to be bailed out of jail every now and then. It's easy to see how important it is to have a good system to track the expenditures on the road. If the system is awkward and not equipped to handle and record all the little details accurately, morale can suffer and the bookkeeping can get all screwed up. This is especially true on the bigger tours, which may involve one hundred or more people, all on different salaries and with different cash needs.

Computers are being used more and more to track expenses and payrolls on the road, making the job of keeping track of many separate accounts much simpler. Advances can be given to members of the crew a lot more easily (See CONNECTION 5.3), because it's no longer difficult or tedious for the tour accountant to keep track of who's getting how much. Each person's account is kept neat, organized, and accurate. Because of this convenient tracking method, cash flow can be analyzed and monitored day-to-day and reports can be sent, via modem, to the business manager back at the group's main office.

Equipment Inventory

For those tours that cross international boundaries, a computer is an invaluable tool for inventory control. Even a stateside tour that might cross into Canada will need to supply the Canadian customs agents with a detailed equipment *manifest*, both going in and coming out. In Europe, manifests sometimes need to be sent out in advance. When an electronic filing system is used for equipment inventory, these manifests (and other detailed reports, such as those for insurance and shipping purposes) can be generated on short notice whenever the need arises.

Telecommunications

Good communication is critical on a tour of any size. On the major tours, contact between the band, its manager, the tour accountant, the business manager (who is traditionally not on the road with the band), the road crew, and other key players must be constant to ensure a smooth running operation. Between the traveling and the hectic and demanding schedule, not to mention the time changes (especially on international tours), communications can be a headache. But with the use of computer telecommunications, tour organizers and others can send electronic mail to one another and avoid the hassle of overseas phone calls and non-English speaking operators, as well as the inconveniences associated with trying, for example, to contact someone in New York or Los Angeles from a hotel room in Turin, Tokyo, or Tucson.

International Management Communications (IMC), The Source, and Compuserve are some of the most widely used commercial telecomputing services or information networks. These services allow anybody with a telephone, computer, modem, and communications software to get on-line (by means of a local phone call) and partake (for a price) of a vast array of information and services. IMC (see CONNECTION 5.5) is the system of choice for most major tours, since its subscriber base is primarily made up of music business professionals, including record labels, promoters, publicity and booking agents, *artist managers*, and musicians. Also found on the network are various support entities such as travel agents, sound and lighting services, trucking companies and freight forwarders.

There's quite a lot to be said for using a computer to communicate while on the road. You can check out airline schedules and rates (even your seats can be booked and confirmed, while on-line), browse through directories of hotels and restaurants in cities all over the world, find out the exact location of the fleet of trucks hauling the sound and lighting gear, or send messages to families and friends back home. But the most important advantage of using electronic mail, commonly referred to as E-mail, has become the modern solution to on-the-road communication between the key players of a tour.

```
      To:    PROMOTERS-US (IMC1500)
      To:    FACILITIES-US  (IMC1600)
      To:    MUSIC-INDUSTRY-PROFESSIONALS-US (IMC1700)
    From:    MENDELL-US (IMC429) Posted: Mon 02-Sept-85 12:50 EDT Sys 42 (66)
 Subject:    POWER & FREEDOM & IMC
```

--More--

Power and Freedom are crucial to any successful business professional. The more Power and Freedom you have, the more effective you will be.

IMC operates the most POWERFUL professional electronic communications system in the world.

We give you the **POWER** to communicate instantly and in writing with everyone on the tour:

..The ARTIST MANAGER from London, the PROMOTER in Sydney, The BOOKING AGENT from New York, The TRAVEL AGENT from Los Angeles, The LIGHTING Company from Dallas, The SOUND Company from Lititz, The TRUCKING Company from Chicago, The BUS Company from Philadelphia, The STAGING Company from Mountaintop, The SHIPPER from London, The MERCHANDISER from San Francisco, The RECORD COMPANY from New York, The CONCERT VIDEO Company from Simi Valley, The AIR CHARTER Company from Los Angeles, The ATTORNEY from New York, The ACCOUNTANT from London, The TOUR ACCOUNTANT from Richmond, and The PUBLICIST from New York..

We give you the **FREEDOM** to make a local phone call and communicate with your customers and suppliers from wherever you happen to be in NORTH AMERICA, the UK, EUROPE, SCANDINAVIA, AUSTRALIA or the FAR EAST -- to wherever they happen to be in any of the above places, 24 HOURS A DAY.

We give you even more **POWER** and **FREEDOM** when you use IMC for incoming and outgoing TELEXES, [illegible] worldwide fares and schedules from OAG; searching UPI and AP newswires; getting 15-minute delayed STOCK market reports; checking the weekly RECORDING ENGINEER/PRODUCER Magazine; using SMARTART computerized ITINERARY and advertising printing services; offering jobs, getting jobs, offering equipment for sale, buying equipment, reading jokes and stating your point of view in an international, professional, electronic, public forum.

If you aren't a member of the IMC family, call me today at our Los Angeles office and request an info pack containing a current directory of our users. It reads like the "who's who" in the music industry.

Join us and experience the **POWER** and the **FREEDOM** of **IMC**.

Regards, Steve Mendell -- IMC, Sales Manager

Disposition: CALL **STEVE** at 213-937-0347

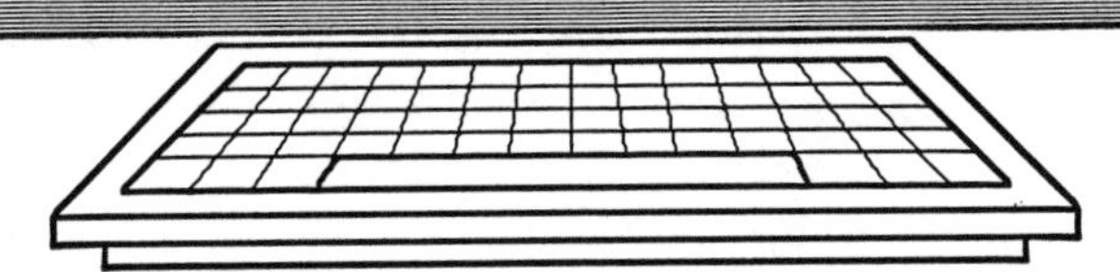

INTERNATIONAL MANAGEMENT COMMUNICATIONS, INC:

183 North Martel Avenue
Suite 205
Los Angeles, CA 90036
(213) 937-0347

254 West 54th Street
Penthouse
New York, New York 10019
(212) 757-0320

78 Princedale Road
London W11
U.K.
(01) 221-2749

International Management Communications (IMC) has over 2000 music biz pros subscribing to their on-line networking service.

One great thing about using E-mail is that you send messages when it's convenient for you and the recipients pick up their messages when it's convenient for them. This is particularly valuable on international tours when it can be high noon in one part of the globe and three in the morning somewhere else.

Almost any kind of document generated by your computer can be transmitted over the phone lines to another computer. For instance, the whole text of a contract can be sent around the world and back again in minutes. Things like detailed expense reports, press clippings, and updated itineraries are a few of the more common documents you can mail out electronically while a tour is in progress.

Ask anyone who's been out on the road with an act and they'll tell you that touring can involve quite a few logistical problems. Like, how can you get three tons of equipment to a location 800 miles away in four hours? Through electronic mail the tour manager can keep in touch with support companies, such as lighting, accounting, sound, and trucking companies, so that everyone who needs any type of special instructions will be kept informed and so that emergencies can be handled without delay.

A road manager or production manager who doesn't want to carry around files on disks can use the network's system to maintain a personal database and access it on a portable computer any time he or she is near a phone. Not only can data be stored on-line, but programs such as spreadsheets or word processors can also be accessed for personal use. This can work like an insurance policy for your data if anything should ever happen to your disks. An added advantage to a set up like this is that other people can access the data from different locations (as long as they are authorized to do so). Storing and maintaining a copy of the tour itinerary on-line is a great way to keep talent buyers, and others with a need to know, up to date.

Some of the telecommunication services offer on-line banking services that allow you to get online with a bank's computer system and take care of banking chores from your personal computer. For instance, you can transfer money between accounts or you can make your regular payments for utilities, loans, insurance premiums, and credit cards. You can also check your account balance, see what checks have cleared, or cancel payment on a particular check. This might come in handy when you're out on the road. You also have the ability to check out your credit card accounts if the card is held with the same bank. At the present time, however, only a handful of banks provide on-line banking services.

Itineraries, Forms, and Graphics

A computer out on the road also plays an important role in developing and maintaining tour itineraries. Press, promotion, attorneys, record label representatives, support crew, and families all need to know the whereabouts of the band at any given point in the tour. Itineraries done on a computer are easy to update. Some of the individuals in a touring entourage only need to know general information (date, time, venue, etc.) while others (lighting and stage crew, for example) require more detailed and specific information. Computerized itineraries (see CONNECTION 7.1) allow for easy manipulation and editing of information so that everyone will be furnished the most up-to-date information available.

Itinerary information can be kept on file in a database and used again and again. A database can be maintained that contains venue specifications (capacity, ceiling height, sound requirements, stage dimensions, dressing facilities, union regulations, etc). Another database related to the city itself (radio, retail, label representatives, promoters, hotels, restaurants, popular sights) can be kept and used as needed. Once this information is recorded, it can be recycled for any future tours. This makes creating itineraries much easier and last minute changes a cinch. Using a database in conjunction with itineraries will make the planning of a tour increasingly easier to do as the database gets more complete.

Using a computer that has advanced graphic capabilities, you can create forms and visual aids to help run things more smoothly on the road. Having the ability to communicate with pictures as well as words can really make a difference when it comes to touring. Maps, diagrams, and well-designed forms for record-keeping, are just some of the more obvious possibilities. We'll talk more about graphics in Chapter 7.

CONNECTION 5.1

TAKING IT WITH YOU

In order to use a computer on the road you've got to take it with you. Let's examine the logistics of doing that. First of all, there are three kinds of *microcomputers*: transportable computers, portable computers and desktop computers.

Transportables (affectionately called "luggables") are self-contained units that are full-function computers. The *screen*, *disk drives*, and *central processing unit* (*cpu*) are usually all built into a case and reinforced for the rigors of travel. Compaq ($1800) and Kaypro ($1,000) are the most popular brands. Some of the models even include a *hard disk* (for an extra $600), which can store all your files and save you from carrying around a collection of floppy disks.

Luggables are fairly heavy to carry around (about 22—40 pounds) and they look bulky. In fact, a concert promoter once commented that the Kaypro reminded him of Frankenstein's lunch box. But for really big jobs, such as tour accounting on big tours, luggables are probably the way to go.

Portable microcomputer systems (also known as *laptops*) are formally defined as those that have their own power supply built-in as opposed to transportables, which must be plugged into a power supply. Therefore, portables work on a plane, a train, in the back of a tour bus, or anywhere else. They may be small enough to fit inside a briefcase and will sit nicely on your lap. Some have disk drives for information storage and some have little micro cassettes built-in. Some portables have a built-in modem and some even have a built-in printer. Grid, Data General, Hewlett-Packard, Epson, Radio Shack, and NEC are the manufacturers of the most popular portables, but other companies are entering the market every day. The fact that portables run on rechargable batteries, and the fact that they are so compact, can make these machines ideal for small and mid-size road tours.

Some portables, such as the Radio Shack models 100 and 200, are not especially good for anything but telecommunications and a few small computing jobs. Their inexpensive price (from $400) and small size have made them the Swiss Army knife of computers. Fortunately, you don't always need to trade off power for portability. The Grid Case, the HP 110 (from Hewlett Packard, $1800), and the DG-One (from Data General, $2600) are all examples of fairly powerful computers that can be used effectively on a tour for just about any computing job that comes up. For instance, the HP-110 ($1900) has the Lotus 1-2-3 accounting software built right into its *memory*. The DG-One has two disk drives and an 80x24 inch screen built into a package that easily fits into a briefcase. But don't let their size fool you. Some of these laptop systems are very powerful — and very expensive. For instance, the Grid computer, with a megabyte (1,000,000 *bytes*) of *memory*, costs $8,000 and was used on a number of space shuttle missions (now *that's* a major tour!).

There are some computers that fall somewhere in between luggables and laptops in size and power. Apple makes the *Apple IIc* ($700), a computer that can very easily be adapted for the road. It's a keyboard, system unit, and disk drive combo all in one light-weight package. There's a portable LCD (liquid crystal display) screen ($200) available, but since the IIc can use any television for a display screen, the LCD screen may might not be a requirement for you. The only other peripherals you might want to carry with you are a modem and a printer. (Yes, there are portable printers that run on batteries). You can buy nice little shoulder bags that can accomodate the IIc and its peripherals or you can probably fit the whole thing nicely into a large briefcase. Beware that the IIc has only one disk drive and is not the powerhouse that the big luggables are. It's perhaps best suited as a second computer to use in communicating with a home base system.

The third type of microcomputer is the desktop computer, which is relatively big and usually contains many separate components. Although it's possible to transport these babies, it's not advisable. Even if you were to have a case made to safely transport a desktop system, setting everything up each time would be a real headache. Another problem would be finding a separate power outlet for each component (i.e., system unit, *monitor*, disk drives, printer, and modem). In other words, if you need a computer on the road, leave your desktop computer at home or work and get something made more for traveling.

One big exception to this general rule is the Macintosh (priced at around $1500). It's a great desktopper but is also quite easy to transport in a travel case (which can be purchased separately). The Mac is a well designed, powerful, self contained system unit, keyboard, disk drive, and screen. The Mac is also easy to set up and light-weight, making it a great candidate for music industry road work.

To find out more about computers for road use, or any other use for that matter, try picking up a few computer magazines at your local newsstand. You may not understand everything you read at first, but hang in there. Almost every magazine tries to include a beginner's column and this is the best way to get started and build some confidence before you start shopping.

CONNECTION 5.2

ROAD MANAGERS AND TOUR ACCOUNTANTS

There are no set rules for the road. Some tours have an accountant traveling along taking care of the money, while other tours leave the finances in the care of the road manager or the production manager. Sometimes a tour accountant is part of the regular entourage, other times an accountant is hired on from an outside company just for the tour. There are even tours, such as those of Michael Jackson and Prince, with six or more accountants handling the show settlements, the concession income, and other money-related concerns. Probably the only thing all the major tours have in common these days is that the bulk of the financial work and the daily organization/logistics are being handled on computers.

Phoenix Management is a company that provides accounting services, including an on the road accountant, to such top-name acts as Billy Squier, Lionel Richie, Billy Idol, Madonna, Rick Springfield, and Def Leopard. Doug McNeil, president of Phoenix, said that his company works with the business manager in developing reports on the tour in progress. "We basically generate reports to help the managers manage the artist better," said McNeil. "All of our reports are generated on a computer and include the dates of the performance, the venue, the promoter, who the opening act was, the capacity, the actual attendance, and other important information that is valuable to the manager and business manager."

The Tour Accountant Management and Schedule package (TAMS), a software program developed by David Cooper of Fox Productions (see CONNECTION 3.2) brings together a series of programs a tour manager can use to keep tabs on the financial aspects of a tour. "The savings of money," said David, "comes in two areas. First, you know exactly where you stand, financially, at any given moment. Instead of carrying around $40,000 in cash on a tour, you can carry just what you need and keep the rest where it can earn interest. Secondly, nine out of ten times, there are so many chargebacks that slip through the cracks simply because the accountant can't track them. The TAMS system can catch everyone's chargebacks. There's no more getting away with nine dollars for laundry at some hotel. It catches everything when the accountant runs the per diem report. The crew hates it." (For more on TAMS, see CONNECTION 5.3).

Mike Page, tour accountant for Hall and Oates, does all his settlements using a Compaq portable computer and Lotus 1-2-3 spreadsheet software. Every evening after a show, Page sends off the night's final settlement to the group's main office via electronic mail. "This process really allows me to get more sleep", said Page, "because our business manager would normally show up at his office at 8:00 in the morning and immediately call me at my hotel room to ask how last night's show went and what the figures were, not realizing that I might have gotten to sleep just three hours earlier. So, instead, I E-mail all the information as soon as I get back to my room, he has it at his desk when he walks into his office, and he doesn't have to wake me up."

John Toomey got his first exposure to computers while on the Hall and Oates tour and has been hooked on computers ever since. He went on to become road manager for blues-rock guitarist George Thorogood and was helpful in automating Thorogood's entire touring organization.

"The amount of time it saves is astronomical," said Toomey. "It's just unbelievable. When I first became involved with computers, working with the Hall and Oates organization, they were using computers to take care of all their bookkeeping, all their income, cash flow, and expenses. I've got to admit, at first I was a bit confused because I was doing all of this manually and I was taught the old route, with forms, calculators and all that. So, I was a little taken aback at first. But then I saw how fast and how basically error-proof it was. And the thing that really stuck in my mind after watching the Hall and Oates people use their machine was the fact that they could do this massive amount of daily paperwork in the fraction of the time it takes to do it manually. I was so impressed, and I thought, this has got to be what's happening for the future."

According to Toomey and others, the computer-aided tour manager can take the place of a tour accountant, thus saving the band and its organization a lot of money. But besides using computers for financial applications, such as show settlements and tracking of expenses, road managers are using computers for tour planning (see CONNECTION 4.1) and the on-the-road logistics of running a tour. "The production manager would use it to do stage diagrams, and to figure out rigging points," said Toomey. "I would use it for guest lists, rooming lists, memos, itineraries and anything else that came up. It really helped the tour manager and production manager in the day to day activities, above and beyond bookkeeping."

Toomey set up his Compaq computer in the back of the tour bus, along with an Epson printer, and was able to print out rooming lists and other correspondence for members of the crew and staff while the bus was rolling. "If I didn't have it," he said, "I'd have to find a typewriter and type it up. Then I would have to find a photo copier and make copies. If there were any changes, I'd have to go through that entire process again. Can you imagine trying to do all that after pulling into a Holiday Inn hotel in Podunk, Iowa on a Sunday? With the computer, a rooming list, for example, is already on a program. I just fill in the numbers and print it out. It made my job so much easier every day. We would be walking through an airport, and George (Thorogood) would meet someone and say to me, 'Put this guy on our guest list for Chicago, which would be like six weeks away. Instead of writing it down on a napkin, which could easily get lost, I would write it down in my notebook, and then the next time I would get on the bus I would put that into what I call my Future Guest List File. When I pull up the Chicago guest list, I will already have a number of people to add, including the person that George met at that airport. It's really an incredible tool for logistics. I cringe at the possibility of having to do my next major tour without a computer."

CONNECTION 5.3

THE TRUCKERS AND THE ROADIES

A production manager or tour manager who is organizing a road tour that will use computers for communication and logistics is going to want to get all the key players automated. This includes the trucking firms that are hauling the sound, lighting, and music equipment from one venue to another. "We're basically using computers to keep in touch with everyone," said Ervin Grinberg of Roadshow, a company that bills itself as a "total tour transportation management company." Roadshow has worked tours for Huey Lewis and the News, Santana, R.E.M., Barry Manilow, Thompson Twins, Ry Cooder, Todd Rundgren and Utopia, *Wayne Newton,* and others. It's one of a growing number of trucking concerns that are using the IMC network in an effort to keep up with the technological changes occurring in the touring industry. "On every major tour we do," said Grinberg, "the lead driver has his own computer and he checks his E-mail four or five times a day. We use it to keep in touch with the production manager and to keep in constant communication with the rest of the people on the road. Sometimes problems arise, and a phone call is necessary. But even after a phone conversation, we encourage all our truckers to get back onto the computer and send out electronic messages confirming the outcome of the conversation, just to get it in hard copy. We're like a command post and I would say computers have upgraded our efficiency one hundred percent."

Roadshow's truckers report their daily mileage via electronic mail, which keeps their records more up-to-date back at the home office. "It's really been a helpful tool for the business," said Grinberg. "I think it's very exciting that there's all this networking going on. It's new and probably still in its infancy compared to the way it will be used in the future. But it's happening, and that's what's important."

Roadies are also being exposed to the technology. One good example is Peter Baynes, a veteran of many road shows, including a series of tours with Rod Stewart which took him through the United States, Europe, Japan, Australia, and South

America. "The best thing a tour accountant can do to gain the respect of the road crew is to use a computer system to handle the finances," said Peter. "It really keeps everything together, and everybody knows exactly what's going on. If anybody on the crew wants an advance on their salary because they're running low on per diems, the tour accountant can bring their file up on the screen, enter the amount of money, and tell that person exactly where they stand. He can also make a good estimate as to how that status will change by the end of the tour. Before computers were used, everything was always done by road managers out of a messy briefcase crammed full of receipts. We'd have to wait until some time after the tour was over before anything was squared away. Now, we know exactly how we're doing at any point in the tour, and we can get what's coming to us as soon as the tour is over."

Pat Caples, road manager for singer Greg Kihn, has noticed that roadies and other crew members are getting a good exposure to computers from being out on the road. "Instead of buying copies of *Playboy* or *Sports Illustrated* at the airport, a lot of roadies are picking up computer software magazines to read on the plane," said Caples. "The crew is getting more and more interested in the technology mainly because it's happening all around them. It's just a natural chain of events for them to move on into computers."

CONNECTION 5.4

THE CONCERT PROMOTERS

Across the country and around the world, concert promoters are automating their office operations. Many are getting into telecommunications by signing up with IMC (International Management Communications) and other on-line networks. Some are establishing their own databases for venue information and availability, and for itinerary purposes. A few of the major promoters across the country, including John Bauer/Media One Concerts (Seattle), Beach Club Booking (Florida and South Carolina), and Prism Productions (Ann Arbor, Michigan), are using a software product specifically designed for the promoter called FOXPRO (see CONNECTION 3.2).

But for concert settlements, where all the band managers and accountants are using computers extensively, the promoters, for the most part, are sticking to their old ways.

"This has really surprised me and I'm really not clear on why promoters are not using computers," said Mike Page, the tour accountant for Hall and Oates. "All the promoters are sitting there going through all the expenses longhand to come up with totals and percentages. Meanwhile, I've dropped them all into the right slot on my computer and I'm twiddling my thumbs waiting for them to finish. Actually, it gives me an advantage. I get that extra time to look over everything in detail and look for problems. Meantime, they're sitting there scratching on paper and banging on a calculator."

John Toomey, recent tour manager for George Thorogood and others, said that many of the promoters he comes in contact with are so uncomfortable with computers that he feels a bit intimidated about bringing his computer into their office to do the evening's settlement. "What I would do is go in with a piece of paper, a pencil and a calculator, just like I've done for the last eight years, and do the settlement that way. When I was done doing the settlement and collecting all the money, I would go out to the bus and at that point enter it into the computer. For me, that seemed to work out a lot better, because I found a pretty fair number of promoters that were really resistant to computers.

Maybe if I had a smaller machine, like a lap model, I would've felt more comfortable about bringing a computer into their office. It was just easier for me, on a personal level, to deal with them using a piece of paper and a pencil."

Bob Peyton is a promoter representative for several concert promoters, including Ken Rosene Presents (Honolulu), Northern Stage Productions (Alaska), and Joe Brown Enterprises (New Zealand). Peyton uses computers for much of his production work, including concert settlements. "The reason most concert promoters are not using computers for settlements," said Peyton, "is that the settlement portion is an art form to them. Most promoters get a real charge out of that experience. Their favorite part of the evening is rolling up their proverbial pant legs, wading in the numbers, and getting into the negotiations. It's sort of like a Monopoly game where everyone's trying to get Boardwalk Avenue. It's not like anybody is trying to pull anything off, it's just that they really like the horse trading. It's very satisfying to them. Some of the promoters believe the computer tends to take the dirt and the fun out of it, and that it makes the process too antiseptic. It's like taking sandlot baseball and putting it into the major leagues. The uniforms don't get dirty on Astro-turf."

CONNECTION 5.5

ON THE ROAD WITH IMC

International Management Communications (IMC) is, quite simply, the premier information and telecommunications network in the music industry. IMC subscribers include nearly 2,000 music business professionals from all over the world. There are other communication networks fashioned to service the music industry, but IMC is the favorite among the legion of individuals and businesses that are using computers as a means of communicating with others in the industry. Besides communication, IMC also provides electronic record storage, access to airline information, various newswire services, printing and graphic services, market research, special interest groups for *digital* synthesizer users and developers, as well as electronic bulletin boards and classified ad listings.

"The system really got rolling because of the folks who were on the road and saw the value and convenience of this type of communication," said Neil Quateman, IMC's director of administration. "With our system, you can basically be anywhere in the civilized world and make a local telephone call to sign on, which then allows you to communicate electronically via electronic mail, telex, mailgrams, or cables. This can be from a hotel room, backstage, an airport, or anywhere else you may be."

IMC founder and president Don Singleton got his first exposure to telecommunications while working for the Westinghouse company in England. In the late seventies, Westinghouse was offered a highly sophisticated electronic communications system, called ITT Dialcom, developed initially for use by the U.S. government. Singleton immediately saw the commercial potential of this product outside of Westinghouse, and this prompted him to leave the company to start his own consulting business. "I was initially going to go after the film industry," said Singleton, "but a friend of mine, who worked for the Rolling Stones, convinced me to go after the music industry instead. He told me that when tours go out, they have anywhere between 70 and 100 people out on the road needing to talk to each other and to their home offices. I'm an educated musician and I knew rock and roll, so I decided to go for it."

For three months, Singleton knocked on the doors of the English music industry, trying to explain the unique advantages of using a telecommunications system. But because his network was merely in the idea stages, he decided to stress the financial management aspects of the system. "What I had wasn't a network at all. I had a tool that I was able to program to control finances. I was using that as a selling point and the communications was kind of an add-on feature."

The first organization that took a serious look at Singleton's system was Hit and Run Music, the London company that manages Phil Collins and Genesis. "You have to understand," said Singleton, "that I schlepped around London for literally three months without any positive feedback at all. It was all negative. There were people telling me 'No, we can't use this' or 'No, this really has nothing to do with me and my business.' But finally, Tony Smith and Andy MacKrill saw it and decided to use it. Just after that, Marcus Bicknell at A&M Records started using it. Then, Adrian Collee at the Elton John office started up with me. And then, John Telfer with Joe Jackson."

But the biggest break for Singeton's networking brainstorm came during the planning of David Bowie's 1983 world tour. "I was called to New York by Wayne Forte' and Bill Zysblat. They took a look at the system, and at first were a bit skeptical, but decided to try it anyway. That's what really made it take off. They showed it to everyone they came in contact with. In the beginning, it was a lot of cooperation from a lot of very good people. But more or less, it was the Bowie tour that made it happen. That's when it turned from a consulting business into a network."

Knowing that 40% of the music industry resides in Europe, Singleton figured that after getting a solid foothold in that market, he would have an easier time bringing his networking vision to the United States. "I knew it would be strategically, a good marketing move. I figured that if I was able to develop a European base, competition would have a harder time driving a wedge in."

According to IMC's Neil Quateman, it was a classic domino theory that got the system rolling in the States. "Essentially," said Quateman, "it started with the road managers who were using it for communications. They're the ones who dragged everybody else in on it. They brought in the production people, the trucking companies, the sound companies, the travel agents, and the freight forwarders. Then the managers were dragged in, and the managers got the accountants and the lawyers interested, and then the record companies got into it, and on and on."

For tour and production managers, the IMC system has turned into a virtual necessity for keeping a tour operation running smoothly on the road. Steve Kahn, who works for Bill Graham Presents and is tour manager for Santana, uses the system to send out the band's itinerary to everyone who needs to know the band's touring schedule. "When we make a change on anything that affects various people" said Kahn, "I can just type it into the system once, and with one command, send it to all the people involved. It comes in handy because I can send off our itinerary as changes occur during the tour. I can just put the changes into the system, and send the information back to our accounting office, our legal office, and our main office in San Francisco. When we start dealing with overseas freight, all of our freight forwarders and trucking concerns are also on the system."

Kahn found the system of particular value when he managed a Bob Dylan/Santana tour through Europe. "Some of the telephone services in Europe leave a lot to be desired. Once we got on-line, it was so much more convenient and really cut down the costs. The key thing in Europe is that all your hotels and travel services have Telex machines, and because we were on IMC, we were able to send Telex messages from a hotel room in London direct to any of the other hotels that we would be visiting."

Prior to the existence of IMC, messages would be sent using the hotel's Telex machine. "You would write or type the message," Kahn said, "and then hope and trust that their Telex operator would send it correctly."

Sharon Weisz, head of W3 Public Relations, based in Los Angeles, has represented such music personalities as Deep Purple, Dio, and Lindsey Buckingham and Christine McVie of Fleetwood Mac. She uses the system to send off guest lists, press information, photo pass lists, interview requests, and other important items while her clients are out on the road. Said Weisz: "IMC has made it a lot easier to be in touch with a band or a band's road manager in a touring situation and it saves a lot on phone calls."

When Deep Purple was on tour, Weisz found the system a great way of keeping in touch with the group's manager. "The manager wasn't always on the road with the band, and when I didn't know where he was, I still had a way to get to him because he checked his electronic mail box pretty regularly. I found that using the system is much more efficient than using the telephone, because no matter how long you talk to somebody, you always manage to forget something you wanted to ask or say. But on E-Mail, you just go back and send another message. Not only that, but it's a lot easier to get definite answers out of people when you don't have to pin them down on the phone. And even when you do confront somebody over the telephone, they'll usually say 'Well, let me think about it and I'll get back to you.' Over E-mail, you can get a real answer out of them a lot faster if they have this direct message in front of them and they can stare at it and come up with a reply. It just makes it a lot easier to communicate with people."

IMC is making dramatic changes in the way industry professionals are communicating with one another, because it facilitates direct and instant access between people. Many top executives are traditionally insulated by five or six secretaries. With IMC, the majority of executive users are either using E-mail themselves or getting a direct print out of messages from their secretaries.

"I call it behaviorial modification," said Janet Ritz, a computer consultant to the music industry. "The music business is a little too caught up in action and re-action, and anything that cuts that down and helps get clearer communication is absolutely necessary. If you're in the music industry, and especially if you do any kind of traveling and you need to be in touch with people outside of the city you are in, using IMC can be a great investment. But it's also important that you're interested in that behaviorial modification in terms of not dealing with people's egos. In other words, you want to start really communicating with people in your industry."

Although IMC saves money and time for its clients, the service does not come cheap. The cost for domestic communication within the United States is about 28 cents per minute. Obviously, when people first get on to the system they're spending more time experimenting, training, and learning by trial and error, which means larger bills during that period of orientation. Getting onto IMC also forces the purchase or lease of computers by music companies and individuals that have not taken the technological plunge yet. Potential users must determine whether the investment involved is relevant to their particular needs. According to Janet Ritz, "most people who are working on a national and international level in the music industry find major benefits from this investment if they use the system correctly."

IMC's effect on the music industry in the past three years has been remarkable. Mike Page, a tour accountant for the Hall and Oates organization is one of many who believes that getting onto the system is now a necessity. "I would say that in six months it will be impossible to function in this business without being on IMC."

CONNECTION 5.6

BOOKING TALENT

The large booking and talent agencies are slowly moving away from dependence on *mainframe* systems and into the more flexible and friendly world of personal computers. ICM (International Creative Management), the biggest talent agency in the world, is in a period of transition concerning the use of computers. Dean Calabrese, Systems Coordinator at ICM's main office in New York, said that it has only been within the last year that the company has taken a serious interest in personal computer systems. "There seems to be a higher computer literacy level among people in general," said Calabrese. "By and large, management is nervous about it, but the line people are thrilled. The company has been somewhat in the dark ages for a while, but I think that's historical with these kind of companies. First we had the systems and accounting people who wanted to put computers in place, and now we have the creative folks who want to become users. So, there's a whole new group here automating, and I was hired to help coordinate that effort."

Right now ICM uses personal computers in the budgeting, scheduling, and planning of tours for its clients. "We have a map of the United States on one system, and we're able to draw lines and determine mileage and travel routes. That system takes into consideration the union regulations pertaining to how far the crew and the artists can travel in a day. We also do all the booking forms, contract papers, and other applications used by our management, on personal computers."

According to Calabrese, contract riders done on a word processing system help to simplify the tedious task of inserting and deleting clauses within contracts that are drawn up. "I look at these riders, and I understand they have to be there, but they're hilarious. For example, the Gregg Allman Band might require so many soft drinks to be delivered so many times a day. They require that they have top billing. They require that Gregg must be spelled with two G's. And this goes on and on for pages and pages. These legal clauses are the wordiest, the most rigid, and the most tedious in terms of wordsmithing, and the computer systems provide a big time savings in this area."

ICM has not yet ventured into the on-line networking aspect of booking. On the other hand, Los Angeles-based Triad Artists, a booking agency that represents Tina Turner, X, Morris Day, Kenny Loggins, and others, uses both electronic mail and bulletin boards to monitor and attract business. Triad now lists many of its touring artist's itineraries, schedule changes, and date availabilities on PAN, the Performing Artists Network (see Connection 6.1).

"One of the aspects that most interested me about PAN was the fact that they were going after colleges and universities," said David Snyder of Triad. "The whole unknown notion of that is very exciting. The colleges are not as sophisticated as they used to be in booking concerts, and with the limited amount of money they do have, they usually don't know how to spend it well. But if they can access a network that can give them concert availability information, and information on the tours that are out there, they can simply respond to those availabilities by sending an electronic message saying, 'We're interested in this act, please give us a call'. Overnight, we can find out whether buildings are available or offers are possible, and what the competition is up to. Those are things that might take us three or four days to do without a computer."

In the office, Triad uses a number of Apple IIc computers for various database systems, electronic spreadsheet programs, and word processing. The company also takes advantage of *Billboard* magazine's on-line chart reporting service, known as the Billboard Information Network (BIN). "We're learning about both radio activity and record sales activity through the BIN system," said Snyder. "We're able to track artist and chart reports a week before the actual magazine comes out. It not only improves our sales ability, it improves our credibility. It's an effort on our part to know something about the people we're trying to sell to."

Chapter Six

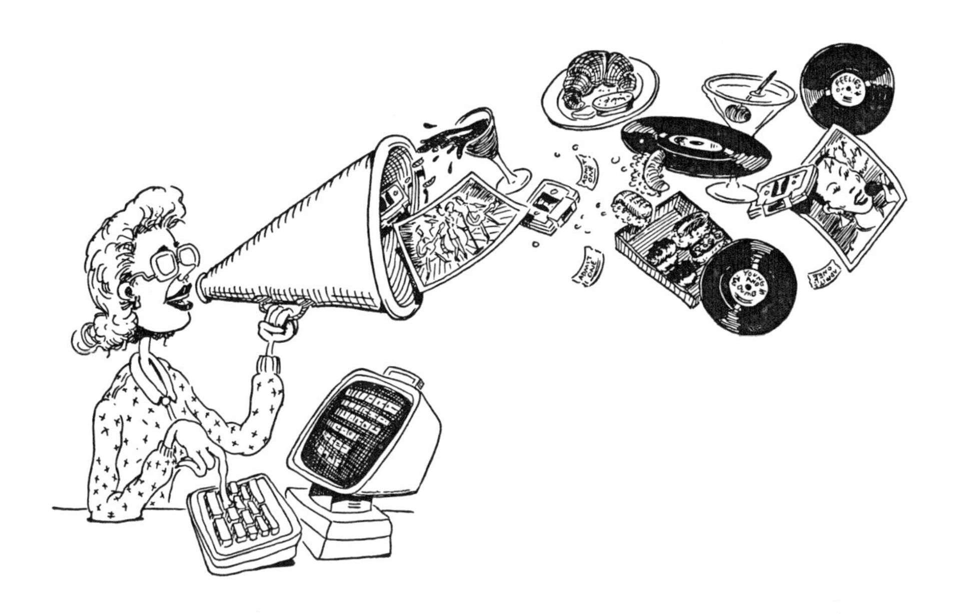

THE PROMOTION AND PUBLICITY GAME

Without promotion and publicity, the word "beatles" might still be a mis-spelled entomological term referring to a particular type of insect. Let's face it, it's not just the music itself that determines success in the music industry; it's the hyping, pushing, and image-making that gets the records played, the videos seen, and the concert seats sold. The industry will always need the stereotypical aggressive, quick-tongued promo person and the personable, smiling, over-worked publicist. Some things will never change. But what is changing are the methods and tools these professionals use to get their job done.

Promo Seltzer

A big part of selling a record to the public is selling it to radio first. A major label may send out as many as 5,000 records as promotional copies to disk jockeys and radio program directors all over the world. The cost of promotion can sometimes be the single biggest cost involved in producing and marketing a record. Some labels handle their record promotion in-house while others hire an outside promotional service. Some do both. Of course computers are being used to help get the records and other promotional material sent out.

Promotional efforts, aided by computer, are not limited to big labels and established independent record promoters. Today, promotion is so important that artist managers and even song publishers are supplementing the record labels' efforts. Computers come into play not only for the mail-outs, but also in tracking all the statistics and phone calling that goes on during a promotional campaign. The gospel of the promotion game, however, is still the mailing or contact list.

A radio station list, for example, would typically include the station's mailing address, the music director's name, and a telephone number. These lists can be purchased or (if you look hard enough) found floating around among friends and colleagues in the business. Mailing lists often come in a format that makes them easy to photo-copy onto adhesive mailing labels, but very difficult to update. Lousy print quality, too.

Today, mailing lists are being kept on computers. Even the simplest of home computers, costing as little as $100, will do an adequate job of generating mailing labels. A database maintained on another more capable computer, however, can easily handle much more mailing list data than a name, address, and phone number. A typical database record on one radio station might include call letters, nickname, *parallel*, region, reporting day, listening day, programming niche (contemporary hit radio, country, dance oriented radio, rhythm and blues, album oriented radio, adult contemporary, new music, etc.), program director (PD), music director (MD), names of DJs, program consultants, reporting publications, and so forth. A database is also easy to update when information changes. Any and all information in the database can be printed out in a list in just about any configuration you might need.

Typing in all of the information about the hundreds of radio stations and publications on which a promotion effort will typically concentrate is sometimes a bigger job than you're willing to take on. Well, fear not. One way to get the information you need is to find it already on disk. Sometimes you may luck out and find a generous soul who will give you a copy of the data at no charge. But if you need to be sure the data is accurate and up-to-date, you might want to contact one of the commercial list brokers who will be happy to sell you the information already configured for your particular computer. One company that specializes in music industry information on disk, as well as in *hardcopy* directories, is Music Industry Resources (see CONNECTION 6.4).

Besides storing the static data on radio stations (i.e. name, address, and phone) a computer system can be used to track the progress of a record from the initial mailing to whenever the promotional effort ends. For every station that was serviced, a chronological file can be kept, along with coded or written notes, on how each station reacts to the product. The following information can be tracked and recorded for each station:

- Have they received a copy?
- Has it been added to the playlist?
- How many weeks of play?
- Rotation status
- Notes on the last conversation with PD
- Next course of action

This "follow up" data can be combined with the static data and you can then generate reports that tell you at a glance how you're doing and suggest what you may want to do next. These reports can also be sent to record labels and distributors, letting them know how specific albums and singles are doing in different parts of the country and perhaps indicating where they can best concentrate their marketing efforts.

Station ______ Report.1 [ ] Report.2 [ ] Format [ ] Code/Rep [ ][ ]

E/L [ ] P# [ ] Ack. [ ] Blk. [ ] Call [ ] Add [ ]

1Address ______ 1City ______ 1St. __ 1Zip ______

UAddress ______ UCity ______ USt. __ UZip ______

Tel. #1 ______ Tel. #2 ______

MD First ______ MD Last ______ PD First ______ PD Last ______

Comm. ______

S#	Single	Testing	Added	
1.				1.
2.				2.
3.				3.
4.				4.
5.				5.
6.				6.
7.				7.
8.				8.
9.				9.
10.				10.
11.				11.
12.				12.
13.				13.
14.				14.

The Dudley Gorov Organization, a record promotion company based in Los Angeles, uses a Macintosh computer along with custom-made software designed on the Helix™ database system.

There are other promotional targets besides radio stations to consider. There are hundreds of local and national music video programs as well as dance clubs and retail outlets that need attention. Everything we've just been saying about radio promotion is applicable to these areas as well.

Compu-Schmooze

The most valued asset that a promo person has is the credibility of the relationships that he or she has built up through the years with people in radio and the press. The computer, even with all its information-handling capabilities, will not make up for a shortcoming here. But when it comes to the extracurricular activities that are part of promotion, the computer can be a great help.

Handling guest lists and invitations for concerts, parties, and other promotional functions is one good application for a computer. You can also have the computer remind you of birthdays and anniversaries, to help you maintain, and enhance, that personal touch.

Meeting people on-line, making and maintaining contacts, networking, and keeping a highly visible profile are some of the little known advantages to be gained from using computer telecommunications in the music business. Music-industry specific networks, such as the Performing Artists Network, (see CONNECTION 6.1) provide meeting and conferencing opportunities on-line, so that people can meet, chat, and perhaps establish mutually beneficial business relationships.

Charts R Us

If the mailing list is gospel in the promotion world, then the charts are just plain God. When we say "the charts" we mean those weekly ratings of the top records and videos listed in the industry trade publications, such as *Billboard* and *Cash Box. Billboard* has gone on-line with the Billboard Information Network (BIN), and anybody with a computer and a paid up membership can access an astounding amount of valuable chart

The Billboard Information Network (BIN) provides chart information to on-line users a full week before the charts are actually published in Billboard Magazine.

information. Billboard's literature describes BIN as an "exclusive computerized on-line database, reporting on the changing patterns of music, as reflected by radio airplay and sales activity." BIN's features include:

- •Access to any of Billboard's charts as much as seven days before the actual magazine hits the newstands;
- •Access to airplay action and Billboard chart sales data in each and every major radio format. Radio formats include contemporary hit radio, country, dance oriented radio, rhythm and blues, album oriented radio, adult contemporary, new music and others;
- •Weekly play lists of individual radio stations;
- •Reports on which of 700 stations in the United States are playing any given title;
- •Reports that track any number of titles over a period of specified weeks;
- •Song title searches by label, geographical region, format, or any combination.

The options available are extensive and, needless to say, most of the major record labels are making good use of this on-line database service. Billboard is ahead of the pack as far as the computer on-line access is concerned, but we suspect other music trade publications, such as *Radio and Records*, to be following close behind.

Meet the Press

Publicists have the enormous responsibility of getting the artist, and the artist's product (be it a record, video, concert, or merchandise), into the public eye and public ear. This is done by communicating and establishing relationships with record reviewers and other journalists. Many hours are spent sending out press and promotional material, setting up interviews, arranging press junkets, and throwing parties.

A word processor, used by a publicist or public relations person, can obviously help with getting out those press releases, bios, and other written material. Drafts for approval can be printed out with ease, so the manager and the artist can make their changes and corrections, and return them to the publicist. Then, the changes can be made without retyping the whole thing.

New developments in computer telecommunications are offering alternative ways to get your copy to members of the press. Services like the U.S. Postal Service's E-com, MCI mail, and other similar services, allow you to write your press release on a word processor and then go on-line and send it to as many addressees as you want. Your text will instantly be transmitted to the local post office nearest the addressee, printed out as hard copy, and delivered with the next day's mail. If time is in short supply, this can save a lot of it.

Information networks through which press releases can be uploaded to a public access area are also beginning to take shape. The press, and other interested parties, can log on to these networks and pull down whatever copy looks interesting to them. This is similar to the wire services, only cheaper. A journalist, for example, can capture the downloaded text, transfer it to a word processor, and use it to write a story, review, or column. Employed correctly by the publicist or the journalist, this electronic press release method ensures accuracy in the published copy. Publicists who use this method can sleep better knowing that names like Yngwie Malmsteem and Andreas Vollenweider will be spelled correctly in tomorrow's newspapers.

Another responsibility of a publicity person might be to collect all the articles and reviews written about a particular group or individual. Now there's a way to gather written press material without even touching a single newspaper or magazine. Most of the major on-line information networks offer their users news-gathering capabilities. For instance, IMC has a newswire feature called NEWSTAB, which will scan, 24 hours a day, through record charts, entertainment columns, feature articles, and news stories for a specified name (like the name of a group, song, or movie title). When it finds the name, the system will pull out the entire item and insert it into the user's electronic mailbox.

The Indie Underground

For the alternative music scene, which includes independent labels, unsigned acts, and small clubs, there is the Performing Artists Network (PAN), which contains databases for clubs, college radio contact lists, retailers, independent promoters, press contacts, and the influential alternative radio play list from the nationally distributed *College Media Journal.* PAN also offers a way to advertise and sell music-related products and services to a large on-line audience. (For more on PAN, see Connection 6.1).

By taking advantage of E-Mail, electronic bulletin boards, on-line conferencing, and what's known as an "industry forum" (where special-interest groups can maintain an ongoing electronic dialogue), an emerging indie underground has opened communication lines that stretch coast to coast. Bands are booking tours (see CONNECTION 5.6), doing advance work, promoting and selling independent records via on-line networking.

CONNECTION 6.1

PROMOTION ON THE PAN NETWORK

The Performing Artists Network (PAN) is an information network that offers a variety of on-line services for the music industry. PAN does not have the high profile, the elite clientele, or the impressive number of clients that IMC has, but the communication and database services available (or soon to be available) on the network serve a viable function for many individuals in the business.

"Most of the systems that are geared toward the music industry," said PAN founder and president Perry Leopold, "are simply electronic mail services, and at the current stage of development, electronic mail is obligatory. The question is, what do you do for an encore? The way we look at it, there are basically two types of services. There's communication, either through electronic mail or teleconferencing, and there's database retrieval, like the BIN network which is totally data-related and doesn't have anything to do with communications, per se. We are trying to integrate the two. Our goal is to make everyone in the music industry a local phone call away from each other."

In the area of promotion and publicity, subscribers to PAN can take advantage of the Press Room. This option allows anyone who has access to the network to submit a press release to PAN's on-line newswire. Before news stories and articles are accepted for release they are reviewed by PAN to make sure they are bonafide, then made available internationally to newspapers, magazines, and anyone using PAN's Newswire. PAN also has an on-line special interest group called Music City that offers information on records, tapes, tickets, books, fan clubs, videos, and other music merchandise.

Another service PAN plans to offer is for users involved in broadcasting. Radionet allows radio stations to electronically transmit their playlists directly to the trade publications and gives program directors, music directors, and promotional people access to those playlists on-line. Radionet is also designed to provide the broadcasting community with a place to comment on the general state of radio. The concept is similar to a magazine's letters department, but the fact that it's computerized will make it much more immediate.

Leopold also plans to develop various special interest networks and databases, such as an electronic booking system (see CONNECTION 5.6), Pro Audio Net, and others. But his main motivation stems from what he sees as the incredible promotional possibilities of networking with other people in the industry, on-line. He takes special pride in the conferencing capabilities PAN provides.

"Our system," he said, "is designed to ultimately give you the ability to attend a music industry convention on a daily basis without ever leaving your office. The conferencing is set up so that, if you wish, you can constantly meet new people from all over the world that you wouldn't have the opportunity to meet in your day-to-day business activity. It's just like at a convention, when you bump into somebody in an elevator and start talking. It works the same way on the system. You may bump into someone in the teleconferencing area and ask 'Who are you?' We have a very nice feature on our system where, on a voluntary basis, every user can keep a profile on themselves. It can just be their name and the kind of computer they have, or it can be someone's whole life story or any amount of information that's related to the kind of work they do within the industry. The people aspect is enhanced rather than downplayed."

But how about the resistance from individuals who are convinced that meeting industry peers, and that the promoting and publicizing that comes with that, is strictly a "people job" and that there's simply no place for a computer? "Of course," said Leopold, "there are those who are leery of computers because they're afraid of the dehumanizing aspect of using them. The pressing of the flesh isn't there. The looking in the eye isn't there. The fact is, they really haven't been shown the advantage. And that's what we're attempting to do. We're saying 'Hey, there's nothing to be afraid of.' It doesn't really change anything. You're still going to go about your business the same way. You're going do your lunches, you're going to pick up the phone and you'll still use your big phone book. But the computer will add to your options, your flexibility, and your efficiency in conducting your business. Plus you'll be making more contacts and your phone book will get even bigger. The more people are convinced that it's not a threat, the more they'll get into it."

A computer enthusiast calling himself Mad Dog uses the PAN network to help run his three music publishing companies and his independent record label, Brat Records, from his home base in Richmond, Virginia. Mad Dog is one of many independent record company owners taking advantage of the remarkable communication benefits of PAN. "The forum on PAN is a great way to meet people, make good contacts, and kick some things around," said Mad Dog. "Some of the information that has been shared includes facts about different clubs around the country. You can find out what the clubs are like, what kind of music they have, whether they have sound and light systems, the names and addresses of local newspapers, and all kinds of other information to help with the advance work and promotion of independent bands."

Mad Dog has made a number of contacts in New York, Florida, California, and other states through the PAN system, and looks forward to establishing even more on-line business relationships as the PAN network builds and expands. Said Mad Dog: "There's a hell of a lot more potential there."

CONNECTION 6.2

AUTOMATED PUBLICITY

It's hard to imagine a public relations firm *not* using electronic mail, database management, and word processing programs. But, believe it or not, many companies in the publicity field still don't.

Let's follow a hypothetical scenario to see just how valuable these tools can be in the world of publicity:

- •A manager of a Boston-based rock and roll band is studying the charts and notices that sales on the group's most recent album have started to drop despite the impressive start it got on the initial release, which was fueled (of course) by the first single and video.
- •The manager thinks that the time is right for the release of a second single off the album. The record company agrees, the song is chosen and the records are pressed.
- •In the meantime, the manager contacts the group's publicist in New York, so that the release of the single can be announced to the press and potentially generate more copy for the group, which would in turn sell more albums.
- •Using a word processing program, the publicist (or an assistant) can write up a draft of the press release and send it by electronic mail to the manager in Boston. The manager can make a few changes and electronically send the draft back to the publicist's office where the changes are refined and another version is created. Then the publicist might want to send a copy of the press release and other correspondence (via E-mail, of course) to the record company in Los Angeles, making sure efforts are being coordinated and the information about the record release is accurate.
- •When final approvals come in, the publicist can then utilize the database of press information. Labels can be printed up for all the trade publications (*Billboard, Cash Box, Radio and Records*, etc.), the consumer magazines (*Rolling Stone, Musician, Music and Sound Output,* etc.),

and the entertainment editors of big city newspapers and influential weeklies in Los Angeles, Chicago, New York, San Francisco, Seattle, Boston, Detroit, and other large urban areas.

With the use of computers, the publicist gets the information out quickly and efficiently. Publicists know that magazines, especially the national periodicals, are usually working a month or two ahead of their editorial schedule. This means that if you want to get something mentioned in the January issue, you better get the information to the editor or writer no later than the end of November. Large mailings, be it press packages or just a typed press release, are much easier to get out using a label-producing database system. Some systems are even geared to print directly onto Federal Express labels.

For emergency situations, where there's no time to print up and mail out a formal press release, electronic mail will allow a user to send information from a computer directly to the United States Postal Service E-Com system. A hard copy of the text, which is generated at the local post office in the area of each recipient, will be included in the next day's mail. New services may even promise four hour delivery.

The Howard Bloom Organization, a well-automated publicity firm, represents many of today's top musical acts, including Hall and Oates, Prince, Foreigner, Kenny Loggins, Billy Idol, REO, Phillip Bailey, Billy Squier, and others.

"One of our clients from overseas urged us to get onto the electronic mail (IMC) system before signing with us," said Linda Bloom. "They definitely wanted us on, and I don't think they would have gone with us if we hadn't. We've found that it's a lot easier to reach our clients using E-mail than it is by phone. Especially the ones that are abroad." Bloom said that the Bloom Organization also uses electronic mail for sending drafts of press releases to its clients for approval. "It's also a very convenient and efficient method of informing and notifying clients on anything that is business-related. In our business, bands are on the road a lot and it's difficult to catch up with them when you're trying to track them down on the telephone. Using E-mail, we don't have that problem anymore."

The company uses a word processing system to produce all written material and it has in-house mailing lists set up on the computer for the frequent mailings that are a part of their business. Bloom finds databases are a lot easier to deal with than rolodexes. "It's a lot faster to get labels printed up now. Whenever there's an address or name change, we just make the update right away so we always know our listings are up to date. As far as efficiency and convenience goes, it really has made all the difference in the world."

CONNECTION 6.3

THE FAN CLUB

Keeping the fans happy is a sure way of keeping them loyal when the next album comes out. This is the basic philosophy of Nightmare Productions, the company owned and operated by and for the rock group, Journey. Among the myriad of uses computers have in the Journey organization, one of the most unique is for their fifteen thousand member international fan club. "The entire fan club," said Irene Sorokolit of Nightmare, "runs on a database system. The computer handles new membership, and membership renewals, and produces mailing labels for our bi-monthly newsletter and for any other mailings that we do during the year."

The company will often do a special mailing to Journey fans in a specific geographic location. "If there's something special going on in a particular area, we can separate and print out labels by zip code, or by city, in order to target those particular fans."

The fan club newsletter is written on a word processor, and ordering and billing of T-shirts and other Journey-related merchandise is handled on a separate database system.

We asked Sorokolit if she could imagine running the fan club without the help of a computer. "Now that," she said, "would be a *real* nightmare."

CONNECTION 6.4

COMPUTERIZED PROMOTION

The Dudley Gorov Organization (DGO) is an established record promotion company based in the heart of Hollywood that has "worked" hit records by Prince, Bryan Ferry, Kool and the Gang, Los Lobos, Tina Marie, Morris Day, and others. Using a Macintosh computer and a software program called Helix (specially customized for DGO by programmer/ consultant Miles McNamara), the company has found an incredibly efficient method of tracking radio airplay of records they promote. "Before the computer," says Neil Gorov of DGO, "we used cardboard sheets that were difficult to update and there was no standard method of logging the information. Now, it is very easy for us to get reports telling us about every single radio station that's playing the record. We can also find out how many of those radio stations have played that particular artist's records in the past. It's made our work neater, better organized, more accurate, and a lot less time consuming."

Augie Blume is another established name in the music business. He worked with RCA records for eleven years, and in 1968 was named their National Promotion Manager. The next year he received the Gavin Report's National Promotion Man of the Year Award for his promotional efforts with RCA. In 1970 he moved to northern California to work with the Jefferson Airplane. He and his wife, Nancy, aided the group in the formation of their own label, Grunt Records, and helped them sell well over four million records and tapes during the three years they were with them.

In 1973, the Blumes formed their own company, Augie Blume and Associates Music Industry Resources, and have been providing independent promotion and consulting services for a variety of clients including Willie Nelson, Waylon Jennings, Charlie Daniels, and George Thorogood. In 1978, the readers of *Billboard* magazine voted Blume the Independent Promotion Man of the Year.

A few years ago Blume's business took on a whole new dimension when he made his first computer purchase. Working from a solid understanding about the tremendous informational needs of the music industry, his company began creating a series of databases. These databases, which are updated every week, have proved to be useful tools for a wide variety of clients. "When I was with RCA," said Blume, "I had them plug the entire list of radio stations into their computers, even though they were not yet using computers in their record division. Years later, when we got our own computer, we decided that we would start plugging in other things as well."

Blume's list of lists includes:

- The Music Business List — This list contains over 3,300 listings including over 1600 U.S. and Canadian record companies and distributors and their key decision making executives. This list also includes national marketing executives as well as major record producers for each label. Also included here are the 70 largest record retail chains.
- The Music Print Media List — Contains all of the music trade publications, over 600 consumer magazines as well as over 800 daily newspapers in the top 250 markets. This list also includes the overseas music press.
- The Music Industry Trade Organizations and Directories List — Over 250 listings of all musically related organizations and directories.
- U.S. Radio — Lists are available that include all musical formats including contemporary hit/top 40, adult contemporary, album rock, jazz, Black/urban, new age, college, easy Listening, country, classical, college, and news/talk formats.

Blume is able to sort and sequence the database information in a variety of ways. "Eventually," he said, "mailing label lists became a big part of our regular weekly business. Now, for example, if someone wanted to do a mailing of all the country radio stations that report their play lists to *Billboard*, we could zap those labels right out. We recently got a call from someone requesting all the daily newspapers in the country with circulations of 30,000 or more. We can also provide a list of jazz oriented publications from all over the world. I happen to be a jazz freak, so I keep track of things that are going on in other countries with respect to jazz."

Blume's clients normally purchase the information from him in label and/or print-out format. But one day Blume got a call from one of his major clients requesting a national radio list and a national print media list, not in printed form but on a computer disk that was compatible with the client's computer system.

"That was a very interesting experience," he said. "It taught me a lot and made me aware of the fact that a growing amount of people out there would prefer to have this information on a computer disk rather than on a set of mailing labels. When it's on disk, you can make changes easily and updating is no longer a pain."

Blume's lawyer has drawn up a licensing agreement so that he will be able to retain ownership of the information disks he licenses, but allow clients to use them and update them any way they wish. "Licensing the information is a means of protecting my business in case anyone decides to break the agreement by copying the disk and giving it to someone else. Further on down the road we will be making these files available on-line. There's no definite arrangement as yet, but we're investigating that possibility now."

Blume has released the California Music Directory, which he hopes will be the first of a yearly series of directories aimed at booking agencies, bands, managers, studios, radio stations and even libraries. "These directories will be of great use to music professionals, as well as to anyone desiring to make music business contacts," said Blume. "About one-third of the people who have bought the directory already have expressed interest in having the same information available on disk. Our activities within the music industry over the years have increasingly moved us right into the high technology area of the information age."

Chapter Seven

GRAPHICALLY SPEAKING

Studies have shown that people remember 50% of what they see as opposed to 10% of what they hear. Consider the example of showing someone a map versus giving them verbal directions. Or how you may never forget a face but you can't quite remember the name that goes with it.

Millions upon millions of dollars are spent every year creating corporate logos. Corporations have recognized that presenting people with a visual image is the most efficient way to communicate with them and make a lasting impression. These firms also understand that a strong public image contributes to a company's overall success.

Because it recognizes the importance of visual communication, the music industry has always put great emphasis on graphic design in the packaging of albums and other products. Today, the music industry is using graphics in all kinds of other areas as well, many of which we'll discuss in this chapter.

The Mac

The term *computer graphics* conjures up images of television commercials where three dimensional, wire-framed figures come soaring at you from every conceivable camera angle. The time is not here yet when you can do these kind of tricks with a personal computer. Then again, it's not that far away.

For the most part, graphics on personal computers have been limited to business graphs such as bar and pie charts and, of course, everyone's favorite pastime, video games. There has, however, been one major development over the last few years that has brought high-quality computer graphics within the reach of the unsophisticated user.

The development we're referring to is the Macintosh computer, by Apple, Inc. This personal computer is way ahead of others as far as graphics are concerned. With a Macintosh, a user who has no experience with computers or graphic design can turn out amazingly professional looking artwork in just a few hours.

Unlike most of its predecessors which are text-oriented, the Mac is graphics oriented. Instead of a green or amber display, the screen display is black on white, like working with a piece of paper. Anything that can be displayed on the screen can be printed out on most dot matrix printers, exactly as you see it on the screen, with suprisingly high resolution. Software programs like MacPaint and MacDraw (both from Apple) make the drawing of simple geometric shapes incredibly easy. Ovals, circles, rectangles, squares, polygons, and straight lines at any angle or any size can be created in seconds. With the *mouse* or some other input device, you can also draw freehand, just as you would with a pencil.

The computer makes it easy to measure, draw to scale, and line things up. You can grab any portion of your drawing and move it about the screen at will. You can duplicate, rotate, stretch, shrink, erase and basically go crazy with any part of your drawing. The program also lets you include display text in your drawings. You can choose from hundreds of typographic styles and sizes. In the same way a word processor lets you change your text around and refine your writing before you print it, these graphics programs let you change your drawings again and again until the perfectionist in you is satisfied.

There are hundreds of possible uses within the music world for this powerful graphics tool. Graphics such as maps, floorplans, and rigging points for sound and lights can be created on the Mac and can even be stored in a databank and transmitted over the phone lines via *modem.* Animation is also an option on a Macintosh, and programs for the story boarding of music videos are becoming increasingly popular. In fact, even serious art is being created on the Macintosh.

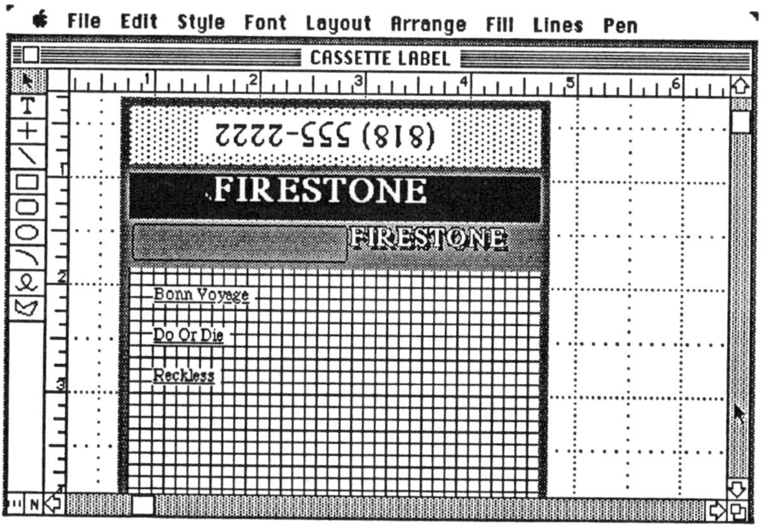

Labels for audio and video cassette tapes are simple to make using MacDraw™ graphics software and a Macintosh.

The new laser printer technology can take normal computer output and create near-typeset quality text and graphics. The laser printer looks very similar to a desktop copier and connects to your computer the same way any other printer would. Since laserprinters are still relatively expensive ($2000-$8000), you may want to let a laserprinting service print your work and send you back (in most cases, 24 hours later) the camera-ready hard copy (see CONNECTION 7.1). With an "electronic print shop," you can send in your printing job over the phone by modem or just mail in a disk.

Although Apple's Macintosh is leading the pack in the graphics arena, others will soon catch up. Already there are packages that emulate and imitate the Mac's superb graphics capabilities. Digital Reasearch's GEM and Microsoft's Windows (for the IBM) and Mouse-draw (for the Apple II) are a few perfect examples. Both the Atari ST line and the *Amiga* also feature excellent graphics similar to what you'll find on the Mac.

For many years this type of computer-aided drawing could only be done on the high priced systems used by architects, engineers, and large printing houses. Now the same capabilites are available in these relatively inexpensive machines.

I Can't Explain

The kind of graphics that a personal computer can generate might be a little crude for certain applications. You might not want to use them for an album cover (although it has been done — see CONNECTION 7.2) or display advertising. But sometimes you'll find yourself in the position where you know what you want from a graphic artist but you can't seem to describe it in words and you wish you had the time and ability to draw the artist a rough sketch. With the computer at your disposal, you have that capability. Better yet, let the artist make a mock up for you on the computer, then both of you can play with different ideas until you decide on something.

You don't necesarily have to draw everything yourself. There are devices called *digitizers* which are attachments to your computer that can transfer the video output of a video camera or VCR to your computer screen. You could, for instance, put a photo or logo (or both) in a computer drawing for the sake of mocking up an album cover or poster. Then you could take a print-out to a graphic artist to explain that *this* is what you're after. Using this method, you can plan layouts of album graphics, photos, advertising, *merchandising*, and even set designs.

Every Picture Tells A Story

The uses for graphics on the road and in the recording studio are limited only by your imagination. Diagrams showing microphone and instrument placement really help when you're on the road and you're using house people that are not familiar with your set up. Drawings that show which wires get plugged in where, can help you get set up faster and with a minimum of errors. Lighting plots, which show where members of the group will stand and how each of the stage lights should be pointed, can also be generated by computer. A drawing of a mixing console, synthesizer front panel, or light board can be created and used to mark down settings that need to be remembered. Diagrams that show track assignments, indicating which instruments are recorded on each track of a multi-track recorder, can also be made up on computer. Another on-the-road possibility is the creation of maps to be included with a tour's itinerary.

A computer-generated logo.

CONWAY RECORDING HOLLYWOOD, CA

SONG TITLE : DATE :

CH # ___	CH # ___	CH # ___	CH # ___	CH # ___	CH # ___	CH # ___	CH # ___
CH	CH	CH	CH	CH	CH	CH	CH
HIGH	HIGH	HIGH	HIGH	HIGH	HIGH	HIGH	HIGH
MID2	MID2	MID2	MID2	MID2	MID2	MID2	MID2
MID1	MID1	MID1	MID1	MID1	MID1	MID1	MID1
LOW	LOW	LOW	LOW	LOW	LOW	LOW	LOW
CH IN	CH IN	CH IN	CH IN	CH IN	CH IN	CH IN	CH IN
PAN	PAN	PAN	PAN	PAN	PAN	PAN	PAN
CH PRE ON	CH PRE ON	CH PRE ON	CH PRE ON	CH PRE ON	CH PRE ON	CH PRE ON	CH PRE ON
AUX5&6	AUX5&6	AUX5&6	AUX5&6	AUX5&6	AUX5&6	AUX5&6	AUX5&6
CH PRE ON	CH PRE ON	CH PRE ON	CH PRE ON	CH PRE ON	CH PRE ON	CH PRE ON	CH PRE ON
AUX4	AUX4	AUX4	AUX4	AUX4	AUX4	AUX4	AUX4
CH PRE ON	CH PRE ON	CH PRE ON	CH PRE ON	CH PRE ON	CH PRE ON	CH PRE ON	CH PRE ON
AUX3	AUX3	AUX3	AUX3	AUX3	AUX3	AUX3	AUX3
CH PRE ON	CH PRE ON	CH PRE ON	CH PRE ON	CH PRE ON	CH PRE ON	CH PRE ON	CH PRE ON
AUX2	AUX2	AUX2	AUX2	AUX2	AUX2	AUX2	AUX2
CH PRE ON	CH PRE ON	CH PRE ON	CH PRE ON	CH PRE ON	CH PRE ON	CH PRE ON	CH PRE ON
AUX1	AUX1	AUX1	AUX1	AUX1	AUX1	AUX1	AUX1
PRE ON	PRE ON	PRE ON	PRE ON	PRE ON	PRE ON	PRE ON	PRE ON
INS 10	INS 10	INS 10	INS 10	INS 10	INS 10	INS 10	INS 10
PAN ∞	PAN ∞	PAN ∞	PAN ∞	PAN ∞	PAN ∞	PAN ∞	PAN ∞
F↔B PRE INS PAN	F↔B PRE INS PAN	F↔B PRE INS PAN	F↔B PRE INS PAN	F↔B PRE INS PAN	F↔B PRE INS PAN	F↔B PRE INS PAN	F↔B PRE INS PAN
___	___	___	___	___	___	___	___

A mixing board diagram, created with a drawing program called MacPaint™ was used for logging console settings .

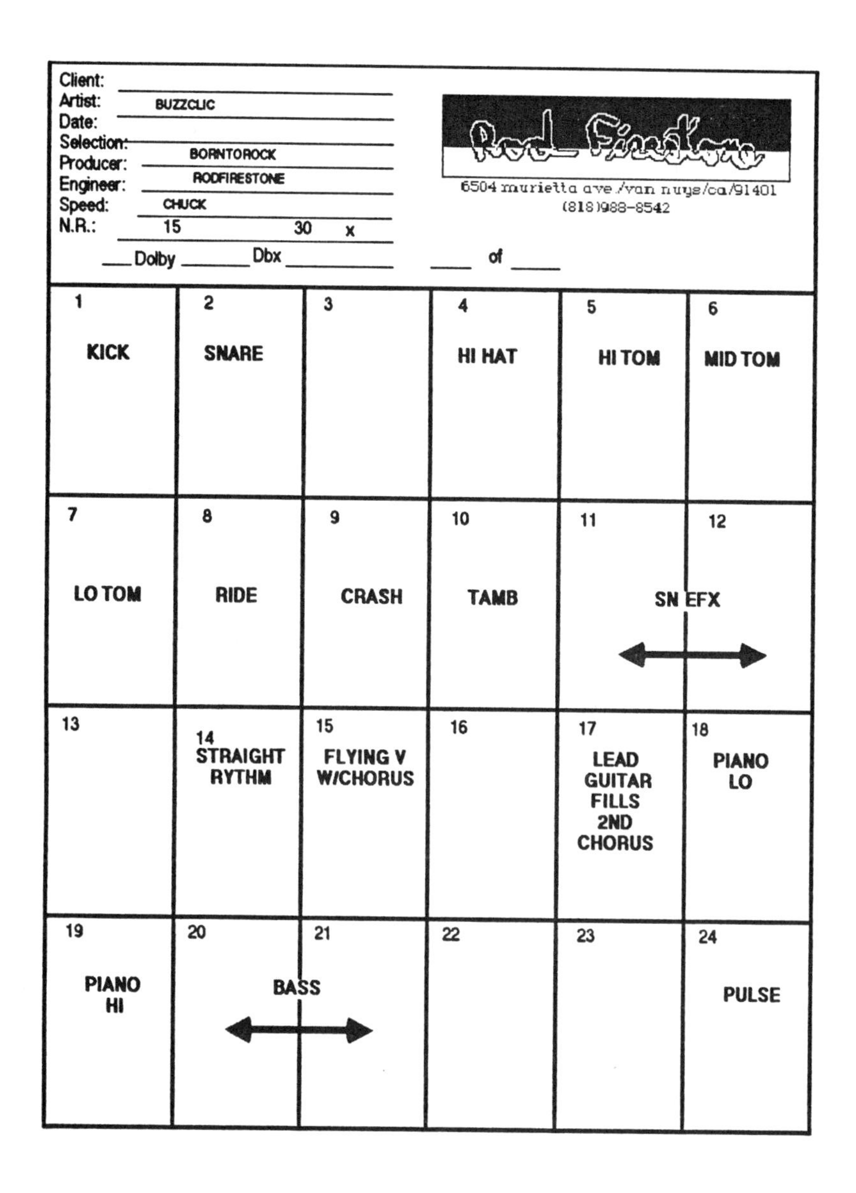

Client:
Artist: BUZZCLIC
Date:
Selection:
Producer: BORNTOROCK
Engineer: RODFIRESTONE
Speed: CHUCK
N.R.: 15 30 x
___ Dolby ______ Dbx ______ ___ of ___

6504 murietta ave./van nuys/ca/91401
(818)988-8542

1	2	3	4	5	6
KICK	SNARE		HI HAT	HI TOM	MID TOM

7	8	9	10	11	12
LO TOM	RIDE	CRASH	TAMB	SN EFX ⟷	

13	14	15	16	17	18
	STRAIGHT RYTHM	FLYING V W/CHORUS		LEAD GUITAR FILLS 2ND CHORUS	PIANO LO

19	20	21	22	23	24
PIANO HI	BASS ⟷				PULSE

Track sheets like this can be easily created using drawing software like MacDraw™ and a Macintosh computer.

Illustrious Output

In Chapter 5, we talked about how convenient it is for road managers to work with a series of forms, created on a personal computer, to keep track of expenses, mileage, and other information. Basically, the advantage of check lists and other forms is that they make things easier for the people working the tour to read and understand information, job responsibilities, and direction. General-purpose forms can always be purchased at your local stationery store, but using a word processing or graphics program, you can create your own customized forms that address your special needs.

Even if you've always felt you were too sloppy and couldn't draw a straight line, with the aid of the computer you'll find youself capable of creating nice-looking, well-designed forms. Sure, you could always get out a ruler and a felt tip pen and make a form by hand, but a computer can do a much nicer job, much faster. The computer lets you start with a blank page and lets you layout a form with lines, boxes, and text anyway you want. It also gives you the freedom to move things around on the page and, when it looks the way you like, to print it out. You can then use the first printout as a master and make as many photo copies as you need. If you need to make a small change somewhere down the line, just go back to the computer, and make the change, and print up another master.

CONNECTION 7.1

THE ELECTRONIC PRINT SHOP

Tom Petty's itinerary for his most recent tour could have been a big problem to organize. Petty's road manager was in one part of the world and the tour's travel agent was in another. The production manager, who also had important information to add to the itinerary, was in yet another corner of the globe. But thanks to a company called Smart Art Productions, (Santa Monica, California), the information gathering, the designing, and the printing of the tour's itinerary came off without a hitch.

"Basically, we offer printing services, on-line, to people in the entertainment industry," said Campbell Hair, who owns and operates Smart Art with his wife Donna. "We use the Macintosh and the Apple LaserWriter printer, and it's turned out to be a real nice way to provide high-quality printing, especially for those going out on the road." Hair is quite familiar with tour logistics having worked for years as a concert lighting technician for Bruce Springsteen and others. "For the Petty tour," said Hair, "all the information was directed to my electronic mail box as it came from all these different sources. Without having to retype it, we (electronically) cut and paste all the information into a database file and then designed the itinerary and a number of forms that they needed."

Smart Art is offered as a service on the IMC system (see Connection 5.5), providing music professionals with a variety of printing and mail services direct from computer (and modem) to print shop. Some of the services available on-line from Smart Art are:

• Mail forwarding — This is an innovative new service being provided on the IMC network for people who do a lot of traveling and have a need to keep up with business and personal correspondence. Smart Art will store letterhead stock and print out the letters typed up by the user over the IMC system. Smart Art will forward the documents to the appropriate party via whatever courier the user requests.

• Letterhead stationery — Without leaving the office, a Smart Art user can have stationery, business cards, forms, logos, and other graphics designed and delivered. Campbell will offer job quotes and estimates over electronic mail before work begins and will even send out rough drafts via courier if necessary. All the work is stored on disk, making it easy to reorder and reprint.
• Resumes — There's no need for an expensive trip to the typesetter. Resumes can be word processed and sent over the IMC network, and Smart Art will edit, rewrite (if necessary) and print it out on the LaserWriter printer. Graphics and digitized photos can be added to resumes, too.
• Custom greeting cards — Besides designing the cards for you, Smart Art will mail them out.

Computer-aided drafting, manuscript production, technical manuals, newsletters, and marketing brochures are also part of the Smart Art service. For touring groups, like Petty, Dire Straits, Sting, Howard Jones, Paul Young, Squeeze, and others, the itineraries can include custom graphics, maps, and crucial venue information and layouts. "Eventually," said Hair, "the information in our database files will be as valuable as our printing service. We hope to have a database access service available on IMC, offering technical and logistical information for the entire music industry."

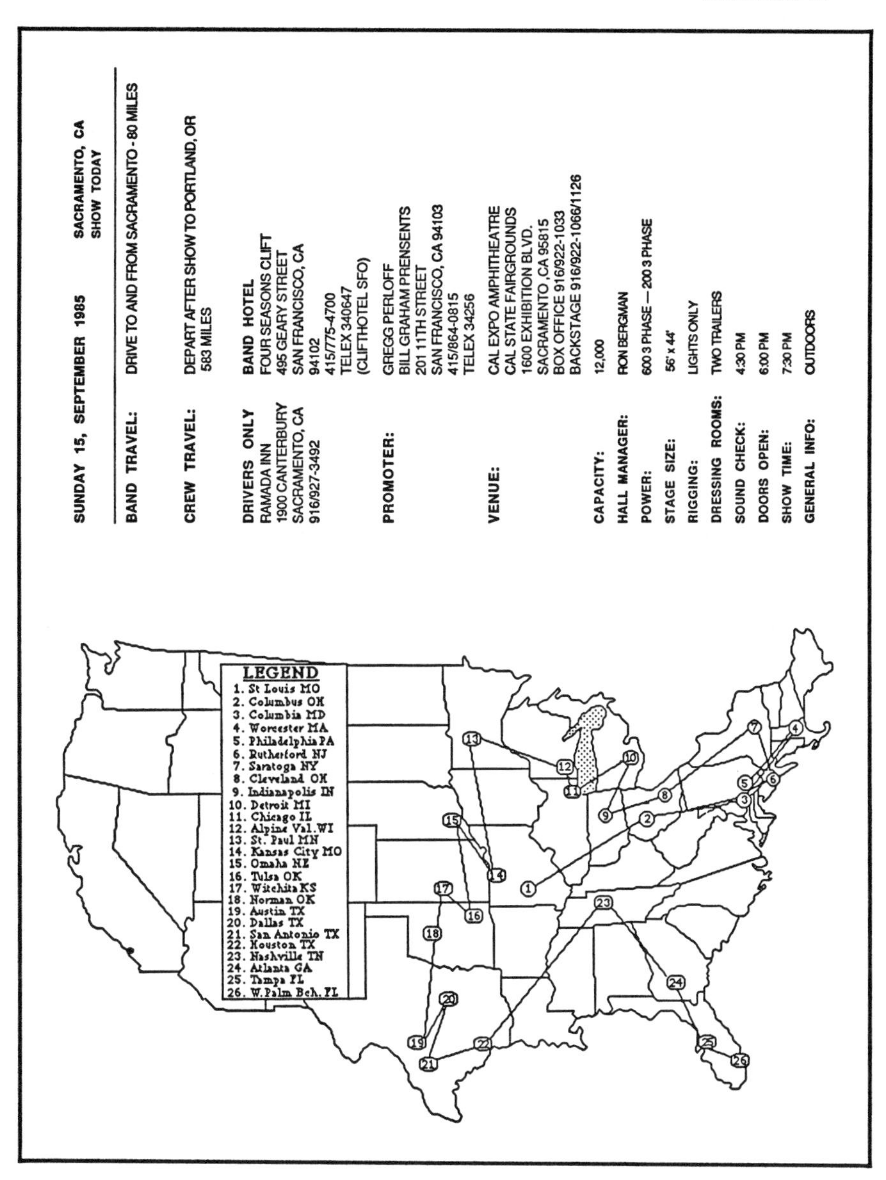

SUNDAY 15, SEPTEMBER 1985 — **SACRAMENTO, CA**
SHOW TODAY

BAND TRAVEL: DRIVE TO AND FROM SACRAMENTO - 80 MILES

CREW TRAVEL: DEPART AFTER SHOW TO PORTLAND, OR
583 MILES

DRIVERS ONLY
RAMADA INN
1900 CANTERBURY
SACRAMENTO, CA
916/927-3492

BAND HOTEL
FOUR SEASONS CLIFT
495 GEARY STREET
SAN FRANCISCO, CA
94102
415/775-4700
TELEX 340647
(CLIFTHOTEL SFO)

PROMOTER: GREGG PERLOFF
BILL GRAHAM PRENSENTS
201 11TH STREET
SAN FRANCISCO, CA 94103
415/864-0815
TELEX 34256

VENUE: CAL EXPO AMPHITHEATRE
CAL STATE FAIRGROUNDS
1600 EXHIBITION BLVD.
SACRAMENTO ,CA 95815
BOX OFFICE 916/922-1033
BACKSTAGE 916/922-1066/1126

CAPACITY: 12,000
HALL MANAGER: RON BERGMAN
POWER: 600 3 PHASE — 200 3 PHASE
STAGE SIZE: 56' x 44'
RIGGING: LIGHTS ONLY
DRESSING ROOMS: TWO TRAILERS
SOUND CHECK: 4:30 PM
DOORS OPEN: 6:00 PM
SHOW TIME: 7:30 PM
GENERAL INFO: OUTDOORS

Using a Macintosh and a Laserprinter, Smart Art Productions produces itinerary booklets that include maps, schedules, and other pertinent road show information. This one is from a Tom Petty tour.

CONNECTION 7.2

UTOPIA

The first record album to display graphics generated on the Macintosh was released in January 1984 by the American rock group Utopia. All of the titles, credits, and jacket information are framed in Macintosh "windows", giving the album, called P.O.V., a high-tech, new-age look. "When I started to lay out the graphics for the record, it was just that — a layout," said Utopia guitarist and songwriter Todd Rundgren. "I was just trying to come up with something simple that would allow us to experiment with a number of different formats. We decided we liked the look of it, so we transferred the whole thing onto the album cover."

Utopia Keyboardist and computer programmer Roger Powell (see CONNECTION 8.2) said that using the Macintosh gave the band more freedom in choosing a typeface and graphic concept for the album. "We were just using it for its marvelous art studio graphics capabilities," said Powell. "Suddenly, we thought, 'Well, no one has done this yet, and someone is obviously going to do it soon, so why shouldn't we do it first?"

Utopia's 'P.O.V.' was the first record to use a Macintosh computer to produce graphics for it's cover.

Chapter Eight

MUSICIANS AND COMPUTERS:

MAKING BEAUTIFUL MUSIC TOGETHER

Our focus in this book has been on the behind-the-scenes business applications for small computers within the music industry. But we also feel that anybody that works in the music field should have at least a basic understanding of the changes taking place in the composing, performing, and recording of the music itself. There's enough going on in this new music-making technology to fill an entire book and whole books covering the topic are on the market. So in this chapter we'll just explain some of the basic principles involved in computer-assisted music creation and raise some issues that are relevant to this dynamic revolution.

The Controversial Sound Of Music

Musicians in the eighties have gone from coveting fine handcrafted instruments made of wood and metal to lusting after sleek high-tech gear glowing red with LED's and filled with silicon *chips*. The search for a heavenly tone has been usurped by a hunger for more *RAM* and better software. Today, a musical piece that would have taken years of study to play can now be programmed into a synthesizer by anyone willing to take a few hours to read a manual. Now when you see a guitar being strummed, you may hear the sound of a flute, and when a drum is hit, you may hear a blast from a horn section. What may sound like a twelve-piece group on the radio or on a record may be one guy with a computer controlling nine or ten instruments. Musicians are now playing *the computer*. It is the one instrument that makes any sound you can imagine — and then some.

Why are musicians doing this? Real instruments sound great. Why mess with a good thing? How could a Chuck Berry or an Elvis Presley exist in this kind of world? What would Beethoven, Bach, and the Beatles have to say about all this? These questions and others like them are on the minds of a lot of people. Some say we should be worried. They say that the group Devo was right about their theory of de-evolution.

The fact is, technology has always brought out the doomsayers, and time usually proves them wrong. When Thomas Edison invented the phonograph, people said it would mean the end of live performances. This idea was expressed again when radio came along, and again with T.V. And oh yes, *again* when music videos entered our living rooms. In reality, each case brought music to more people and made *more* work for musicians. The end result was that the music industry grew as a whole.

Once more, history repeats itself. This time it's computers that are taking the rap. Some musicians are gung ho for the new technology (see Connection 8.3) and some won't have anything to do with it, fearing that the trend marks the beginning of the end of musical creation as we know it. Even some of the music instrument merchants, who are supposed to be a reliable source of information, seem baffled and confused (see Connection 8.1). A lot of this resistance can be traced to a basic fear of the unknown.

It would be an over-reaction to assume that traditional forms of music and musical instruments might become extinct because of the new technological developments. It's just not true. The new wave of instruments and sound synthesizers will not replace the old. They'll simply add to the choices available. Musicians and music lovers alike will soon come to think of computers as just another musical instrument.

The computer has now become a new and versatile tool for musicians and, as a consequence of its use, some of the methods by which sounds are produced are being changed. The beautiful sound of music will remain, as always, in the ears of the beholder.

The MIDI Standard

The revolution we're talking about is usually summed up in just one word — *MIDI*, which stands for Musical Instrument Digital Interface. MIDI is not a gadget or a piece of *hardware*. It is a standard way of doing things. It's like a language or rules to a game. All the manufacturers of synthesizers sat down one day (actually, one year) and agreed to build their future products according to the MIDI standard. Now any MIDI instrument can talk to a computer or any other MIDI instrument.

In fact these digital instruments are nothing more than *dedicated* computers. That is, they are computers made to do one particular job — make sound. Like other computers, they deal with information in a digital form, or more precisely, in zeros and ones. When you hit a key on a standard computer typewriter-like keyboard, it instructs the computer to put a letter up on the screen. Likewise, a key struck on a synthesizer's piano-like keyboard instructs the computer inside to sound a particular note.

By means of a MIDI cable that plugs into the back of each MIDI instrument, one synth (that's short for synthesizer) can control numerous other synths. For instance, if Synth 1 and 2 were hooked together and you hit a C note on synth 1, the same note will simultaneously be played on synth 2. This is the simplest example of a MIDI hook up. Upwards of fifteen synths, all emulating different instruments, can be connected in this manner to produce MIDI symphonies.

The MIDI standard can also be used to store all the parameters of a particular sound. This is known as a *sound patch.* It might be a bass sound, a piano sound, or the synthesized sound of an ocean wave. The sound itself is not recorded in the same way that sound is captured on tape. Instead, the computer instructions (MIDI data) that tell the synth what settings it needs to reproduce that particular sound are remembered. This MIDI data can be stored on cassettes or disks like any other computer information. Storing these sound patches on disk or tape is a lot more convenient and efficient than writing down settings and twiddling a lot of knobs, especially in a live situation. In this way, a musician can keep a library of original sound patches and can even get patches from other sources, such as a friend or an on-line synth network (see Connection 8.4).

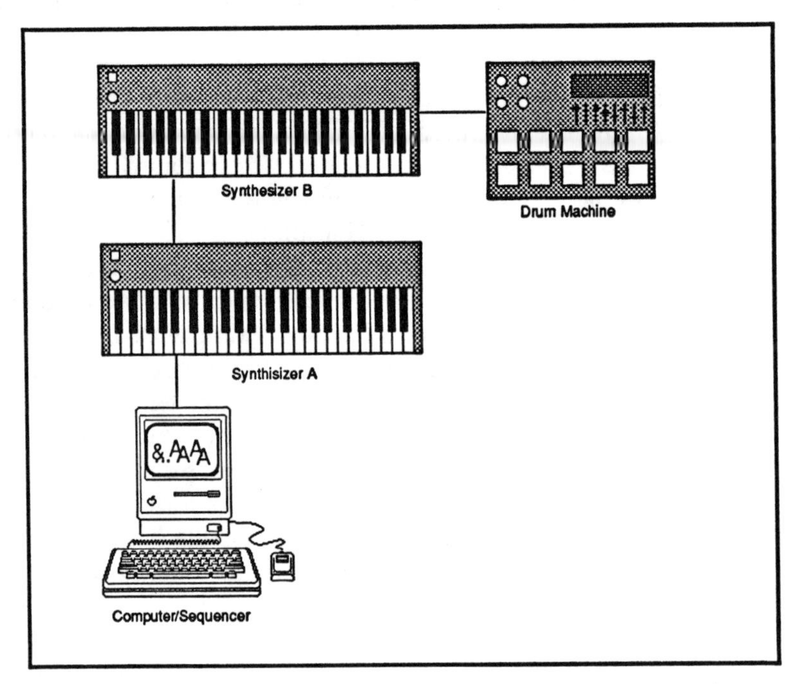

Here's a typical MIDI configuration between computer and synthesizers.

The musicians who use MIDI are generally ecstatic about its capabilities and potential. Many say that there are still problems concerning its overall standardization. Although MIDI is an interface standard by definition, instrument manufacturers interpret that standard in different ways. To the trained ear, there is sometimes an irritating time delay in the sound when two instruments, made by two different manufacturers, are hooked up together. This is due to a lack of standardization between the manufacturers. We're hoping that, as MIDI gets more popular, these issues will be addressed by the manufacturers so that industry "standards" become truly standardized.

Free Samples

Another innovation that the new technology has brought to the music world is sampling, which, in essence, is digital recording. Digital recording differs from traditional (analog) recording in that the sound is converted and stored as digital information (the old zeros and ones again).

Sampling makes it possible to record any real sound and play it back *polyphonically* from the keyboard of a synthesizer. The sound of a Stradivarius, a tuba, or even a car crash can be sampled. Sampling also allows a *drum machine* to produce drum sounds indistinguishable from that of a real drum set.

Converting sound to digital information that can be manipulated by a computer gives the musician an opportunity to experiment with the sound. For instance, the sampled sounds of a car crash could be combined with the sound of thunder for an interesting snare sound. It's not exactly our idea for a ballad, but it can make for great sound effects at your next Halloween bash.

The Tapeless Studio

MIDI and sampling techniques are having a great impact on the recording process. Instead of using microphones and multitrack tape machines to record a performance, a MIDI *sequencer* is used. A sequencer does not record the sounds the instruments make. Instead it remembers the sequence of MIDI instructions and plays them back. Think of how a player piano works and you'll get the idea. To play back a performance on an eight track sequencer, for instance, you would need eight instruments present to receive and playback the instructions. Some keyboards and drum machines have sequencers built-in. It's also possible to add a sequencer on as a separate component. With the help of special software it's even possible to turn a personal computer into a sequencer (see CONNECTION 8.2).

Having the MIDI technology available in the studio can increase the efficiency and productivity of the recording process. When using MIDI, there's no need for microphones, tapes, tape machines, or a sound proofed room. The sound of an instrument can be changed instantly, the tempo of a performance can be changed without effecting the pitch (this is impossible when a performance is recorded on tape because of what is known as the "chipmunk effect"), and when *bouncing down* tracks, there's no loss of fidelity.

A MIDI studio is a great tool for pre-production because it provides a method for musicians to re-arrange, edit, and otherwise refine their composition, prior to committing anything to tape. Many professional recording studios, in fact, are finding their more traditional, multi-track, sound-proofed studios becoming less popular and are now adding MIDI rooms to their facilities.

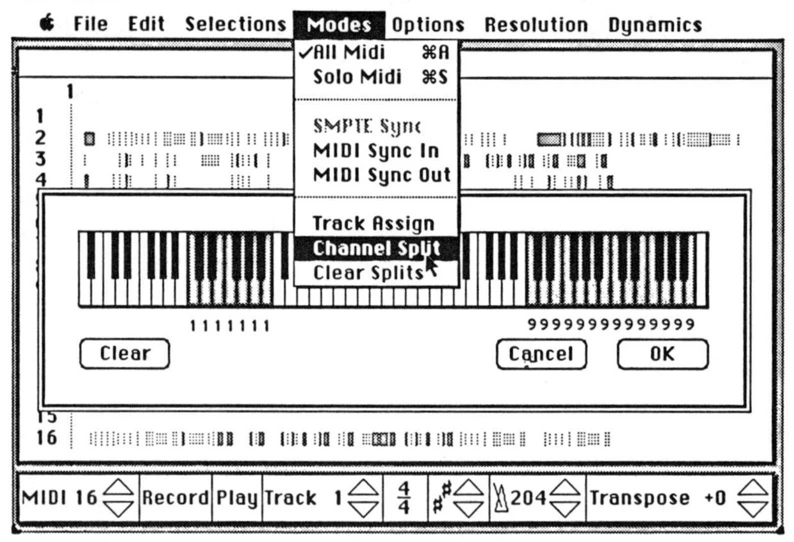

Total Music™ by Southworth Music Systems Inc.

The Future

MIDI is just the beginning of a brave new world in music that's taking shape, and we can only guess about some of the developments that lie ahead. The ability to convert any sound into digital information, which can then be manipulated by a computer, will change the way music is composed, performed, recorded, marketed, and enjoyed.

One exciting development has already been tested by a handful of professional musicians involved in a trans-continental recording session. In this session, two studios, by way of a satellite hook-up, made it possible for members of the band to record their respective parts while separated by thousands of miles. Because of the new technology, they were able to complete their session almost as if they were sitting in the same room.

Sometime in the future, we'll also be seeing inexpensive multitrack digital recorders and studio effects gear made as compact and portable as your standard video cassette recorder. Once such devices are available, musicians will be able to do studio quality recording in their home (or garage) instead of spending tens of thousands of dollars to rent a professional recording studio. Along with the smaller sizes and cheaper prices, we might also get some outrageous features. We may soon see the day when a computer can actually correct a singing voice. No matter how off-key or horrible a voice is, a computer might be able to make digital corrections, giving everybody a chance at music stardom.

Maybe one day, we'll even have the ability to translate our *thoughts* into MIDI data. We might be able to hum (or think) a melody, and it will come out on the instrument of our choice. Who knows? There might eventually even be an "intelligent" computer that can guess at national tastes and trends and compose a number one song.

The way we purchase music may change, too. We may see a dial-up service for home computers that we could use to select the titles we want. The songs would be downloaded as digital information into our home entertainment systems that could play them back in perfect fidelity.

It's hard to say exactly what changes we'll see or what impact these changes will have on the music industry. What is certain is that, as with all technological developments, there will be controversy, debate, and unresolved legal issues to grapple with.

Music seems to be something that man cannot do without. So does technology. Fortunately, these two exclusively human by-products have complemented each other through the ages. It stands to reason, therefore, that despite our inevitable resistance to change, music and technology will continue to coexist harmoniously.

CONNECTION 8.1

THE MUSIC MERCHANTS

It's becoming a classic scenario: A musician reads and hears all about MIDI-equipped synthesizers, personal computer interface with instruments, graphic depictions of music, and all the other technological advances in the making of music. The musician heads on down to the local music store, hoping to learn more and maybe even get some hands-on experience before investing in some of the new gear. But there's a big problem. The store's salespeople are knowledgeable about the electronic keyboards and other instrumentation, but they know absolutely nothing about the computer hardware and software that the instruments work with. In fact, the store doesn't carry any computer equipment at all. Desperate to figure things out, the musician goes to a computer store. There the musician is faced with the reverse situation. The salesperson knows all about computers and would be glad to sell our hapless musician a spreadsheet program, but is at a loss when it comes to how musical instruments can be used along with the computer systems. What's a musician to do?

Most music stores have been slow to accept and understand the new technology. Not only are many store owners, managers, and sales people uneducated about computers, many are also unfamiliar with the features and capabilities of the sophisticated electronic instruments that they carry in their stores. Fortunately for musicians, the National Association of Music Merchants (NAMM) has recently embarked on an aggressive campaign to educate and guide merchants into the new computerized age of music. Paul Bugielski, President of PSC Management Consultants, has been hired by NAMM as a consultant to coordinate these efforts. "The way a lot of music merchants perceive computers," said Bugielski, "is that you push a button and you automatically turn into Beethoven. This false perception is fostered by a long-standing belief that in order for music making to be considered 'legitimate' it must be preceded by years of sweat and practice. The application of computers in music is misunderstood, and is perceived as a threat because there is the potential to short circuit this traditionally long learning curve. The project I have with NAMM is to dispel a lot of these myths and misconceptions."

Bugielski believes that many music merchants throughout the country view the computerized music phenomena as a threat to their industry. "The same thing happened," he said, "with the introduction of the player-piano around the turn of the century. A lot of people thought that these piano rolls would eliminate the need for piano players. It happened again when radio was first introduced. People immediately assumed that no one would go out to see music performed live anymore. They look at computers in the same way. What they don't yet realize is that computers will fundamentally change the way people think about and interact with music which, in turn, will have a direct effect on why they buy and how they use musical instruments in the future. Depending upon who you are, and at what level you want to interact with music, the computer will be able to assume the role of toy, tool, or appliance. Computers will enhance music making, learning, and listening. It's not going to replace existing musicians. In fact, it's going to open up music to a much larger audience."

According to NAMM's Executive Director, Larry Linkin, the annual NAMM conventions have been displaying more and more computer gear each year, with companies like Apple, Yamaha, Roland, Linn, Kurzweil and others making great efforts to reach skeptical retailers. "It's a very important aspect of our business these days," said Linkin. "Part of the problem is getting personnel to accept and understand the new technology. Any store owner or manager is totally dependent on the people they have working for them. A lot of the sales personnel are great at selling pianos and organs, but that doesn't mean that they're great at selling electronic keyboards and the MIDI-interface equipment. Fortunately, this stuff has been creeping up at recent trade shows, allowing dealers to hang out and try to figure out how they can take advantage of this new technology in their individual marketplaces."

The computerization of music is obviously causing confusion, as well as controversy, in the business. Linkin recalls similar industry rumblings in the mid-sixties after the Beatles and other bands set new standards in instrumentation. "Drums were built much bigger and stronger after the Beatles. They had to be because of the different beat and the different style of playing. The same with guitars. We had new designs, new colors and a lot more devices and accessories. But they were still basically guitars and drums. They just looked better and sounded better. It's the same thing with keyboards. Electronic keyboards are still keyboards. They just opened everyone's eyes to the excitement of change."

Reports on the most recent NAMM shows indicate that the interest in music-related computerization is certainly up from previous years. But the retail music industry in general has yet to embrace the new technology as the definitive wave of the future. The reasons vary. First of all, traditionalists among musicians are often insulted by electronic performance and composition. Second, the conventional instrument dealers are often baffled by MIDI and other musical advancements. And, finally, despite its bold efforts to bridge the two schools of thought, NAMM is moving cautiously.

NAMM's caution at one of their recent shows could be seen in the way the convention floor was laid out. Many of the software companies were placed in a seperate building from the rest of the exhibitors. "Any time you start something new," said Linkin, "there's always a growth period. You're not born and immediately able to walk. You have to crawl first. I think we're probably crawling right now, and we're just trying to get up so we can move a little faster."

CONNECTION 8.2

MUSIC SOFTWARE

For the past twelve years, Roger Powell has been the well-respected keyboard player for the rock group Utopia, a rock band featuring Todd Rundgren. Besides touring and recording with Rundgren and Utopia, Roger has taken periodic sabbaticals from the band to work on solo albums or to tour with rock legend David Bowie.

Powell has also spent a good deal of time at another kind of keyboard. Through trial, error, and creative instinct, he has helped pioneer the advent of personal computer musical software. Back in the early seventies, he learned all he could about computers and *programming*, and then went on to invent a hand-held keyboard instrument, called the Probe. He also designed his own digital synthesizer.

Today, besides continuing to be a part of Utopia, Powell is director of product development for Cherry Lane Technologies. One of the company's products is a program called Texture. Written by Powell, Texture offers easy, flexible editing and manipulation of musical data.

Essentially, Texture is the superior alternative to a multi-track tape recorder because it allows a tunesmith to compose music, and make changes in that music, prior to commiting the composition to tape. "Texture is a production tool for musicians," said Powell. "Let's say that you compose film soundtracks and you want to do your composition at home, before going in to record at an expensive studio. This program will allow you to compose the music in your own home with just a handful of keyboards and a personal computer. After getting all your pieces together and editing them on the computer, you take it to the studio, punch a couple of buttons and it all plays back as you've composed it. I tried to give some personality to this program because, besides being a programmer, I'm also a user. A very impatient user. I wanted the program to be somewhat humanized, and I wanted it to address the problems that musicians have to face when they're composing. Having all the

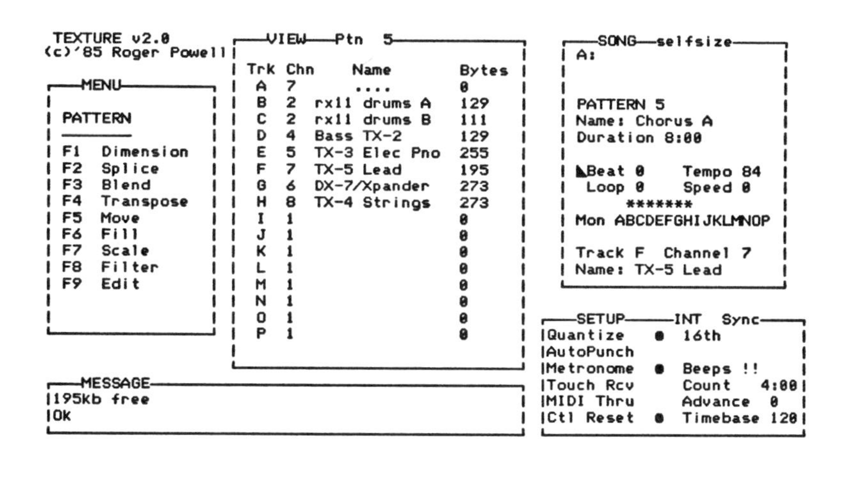

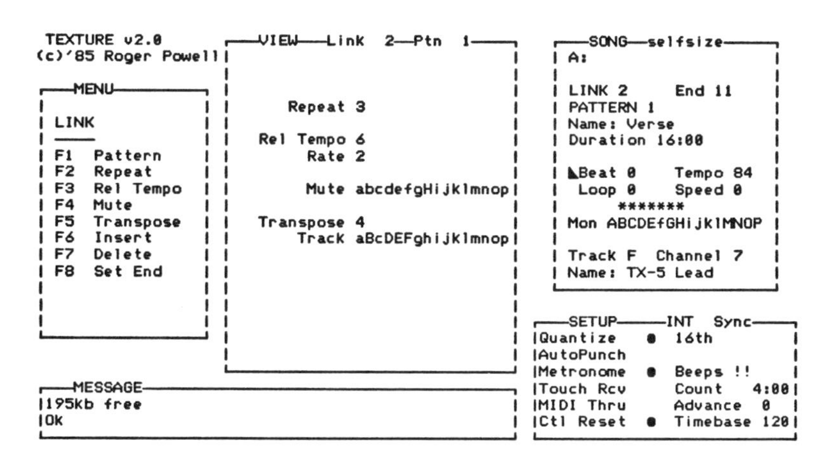

Roger Powell's Texture is a computer program that's used as a versatile production tool for professional tunesmiths.

experience that I have had with recording and composing, I designed a program which represents a process of working that is very streamlined. In other words, you can move around in this program extremely fast and all the operations are performed more or less instantly."

The program allows a composer to change each individual note in a composition, change the key that the music is played in, and slow down or speed up the tempo without affecting the pitch. It even allows the user to have segments of the composition played on different instruments than they were originally programmed for.

"Using Texture, you can record on what appears to be eight tracks, just as if it were a multi-track tape player," explains Powell. "But the program is not actually recording the sounds that you play. Rather, it's recording a list of keys that were pressed and the times when those keys were depressed. This is called 'event data.' Once you have the event data stored in the computer's own memory, you have the ability to manipulate the music in any way."

Texture is designed not to place an additional financial burden on the user for added hardware or memory. Versions of the software are available for the Apple IIe and the IBM PC. Another version is planned for Commodore's new Amiga computer, which Powell calls the "perfect music machine" because of it's highly sophisticated design and its relatively low price tag ($1750).

Another company that develops and markets software for musicians is Music Data. Ron Wilkerson, Music Data's president, said that his company offers about 40 different products, including a line of data cassettes and disks that hold synthesizer sound patches originated by such well known musicians as Steely Dan/Doobie Brother Jeff Baxter, former-Doors keyboardist Ray Manzarek, infamous British session player Nicky Hopkins, Berlin's Dave Diamond and respected drummers Carmine Appice and Denny Siewell.

"Most musicians really don't like to program," said Wilkerson. "That's why we think there's a big market out there for pre-packaged sound patches. Musicians can now buy these patches on disk and download the sounds from their computers into their instruments. That way, a musician can play the keyboard, without having to know the physics of programming. The whole idea behind this is to make life a lot easier. The computer can control all the electronic functions, leaving the musicians to handle what they do best, which is playing."

A second generation of more powerful, yet easy-to-use, MIDI software is now becoming available. One of these new programs is a product called Total Music. Developed by Southworth Music Systems, Total Music runs on the Macintosh. According to Southworth's Paul Lehrman, the package can let professional arrangers, composers or studio musicians "work out all their parts and orchestrations at home, saving many hours and thousands of dollars of expensive studio time. With Total Music, the Macintosh virtually becomes a multi-track recording studio, with precise control over every musical note."

Music software continues to evolve as synthesizers get more sophisticated and as personal computers get easier to use. "We're still very early in the musical software game," said Powell. "The hardware standard that's made it possible to develop useful software is only a couple years old, and people are just beginning to realize its availability. I see the direction of musical applications going pretty much the way that business software has gone. When computers first came out, you had stand-alone word processors, stand-alone data base managers, spreadsheets, and graphics. Now you have integrated packages that do it all. The same thing is starting to happen with music software where we're attempting to centralize the editing and the storage of all sound data. But it's important to remember that a computer does not substitute for creativity. There's no guarantee that when you use these programs you'll immediately write a hit record. They're merely tools to assist and accelerate the creative process."

CONNECTION 8.3

THE MUSICIANS

"I have waited my entire life for this to happen," said musician Dave Bluefield about MIDI capabilities. "We call it music processing, which is basically like word processing in that you have the ability to create any kind of possible sound combination, and it's always in the state of broadcast quality for a recording studio."

Bluefield runs his own company, Bluefield Music, which produces music for commercials and music videos and provides services including background effects, arrangements and composition. Like other musicians who share his enthusiasm for MIDI, Bluefield is excited about the new interface capabilities that are now available for the Macintosh and other personal computers.

"This has been the major breakthrough in the 80's," he said. "A guy like me can play something on a keyboard and maybe not lock into something that's magical until the twentieth bar. Now I can snip out my first nineteen bars and make the twentieth bar my first. I can change the speed or the dynamics, and I can even go in and isolate a note that I don't want and immediately fix it up. It allows me to explore, experiment, and expand in ways that I'd never dreamed possible."

Gary Rotger, a successful New York studio musician who has immersed himself into the world of computerized music (see Connection 8.4), has seen computers as incredible time saving devices for many musicians. "In the old days," said Rotger, "if I was introducing a new song, the band or section I was working with would have to learn the song, rehearse it, run through it two or three times in the studio and then lay it down on tape. With the computer, I can get the basic ideas down and then edit various parts at the speed of light. As I get into it and work with it, I find that the whole creative process can go very fast. With the use of a computer, good software, ten or twelve different keyboards and a drum machine, I can do all of my pre-production work at home, before I actually go to the studio to lay down tracks. This is very cost effective. This allows me to get out all the bugs and make sure the music is exactly the way I want it. Then I can book some studio time and basically just push a button, and it all goes to tape."

But how about the skeptics? How does Rotger respond to people who say that the computerization of music is dehumanizing the art form? "It's just another way of expressing what I want to express. What difference does it make what road you choose to get your point across? It doesn't matter if you're conducting a thirty piece orchestra or you're conducting fifteen synthesizers. The important thing is that your musical ideas are being communicated. People have to realize that the musicians who are taking advantage of this technology are simply using a different tool to express themselves. Music, whether created on an acoustic guitar or a computer, is just another form of human communication. I think one of the fears today is that you will wind up with sterile mechanical sounds if you use machines. This is just not true. Remember, machines are just an extension of man and they have their place. We just have to get use to them."

Keyboardist Tom Hensley has played piano and organ behind Neil Diamond for more than a decade and was responsible for getting Diamond's management company interested in and involved with computers (see Connection 2.1). "Using a computer has become very important in the studio," said Hensley. "A few years ago, it was wonderful to have good sounding demos that I produced in my garage on my eight track recorder. But that was it. I couldn't go any further with the work that I put into a demo. Now, the work that I do in my garage becomes part of the work that I do in the studio. I just take my equipment into the studio and dump my material into the twenty-four track machine. The time I spend in the garage is no longer wasted."

Hensley had been using a program called Doctor T's Sequencing Software on his Commodore system, but is now using the Total Music package with his Macintosh. "Working on other systems is real drudgery after dealing with the Mac," he said. "The Macintosh has definitely spoiled me."

Despite his heavy involvement with computers as a professional musician, Hensley is sometimes overwhelmed with all the advancements and can empathize with some of his peers who have not embraced computers like he has. "I always get a mixed feeling when I see the latest technological wonders because, on the one hand, it's inspiring to experience the power of what you can do with this equipment. On the other hand, it's a little depressing because it's so easy to play that, practically anyone can do it. I'm talking about the whole concept of playing chops and seeing how fast you can play and how advanced your harmonic conception is. That's something that people like myself would like to think that we're good at. But all that kind of goes out the window, and what becomes more important is using your ears to make decisions about what you leave in and what you take out."

Utilizing computers and synthesizers on stage during performance is another area that Hensley has recently explored. "It enables a keyboard player, a drummer, or a guitar player to play more instruments at one time. It's like getting extra hands and extra arms. But it's hard to define how much sequencing one is willing to accept in a performance situation, because you have to play the same thing at every show. That can sometimes inhibit spontaneity by preventing you from doing certain things that you might want to do."

Guitarist Todd Rundgren has been using computers in many facets of his music career, including a series of solo concerts in which he worked with an assortment of sequencing devices spread across the stage. Rundgren also released an album, called 'A Capella,' where every sound heard was created by his own voice programmed through a machine called the Emulator II.

Although he currently uses a Fairlight synthesizer as a song composition tool, Rundgren has become skeptical about depending too heavily on the use of automated devices on the stage. "It tends to take the identity out of the band," he said. "The last time we used tapes (pre-programmed music), it wasn't as much fun as just playing. The only real advantage to all this technology is to make music composition a more liberated and interactive process."

CONNECTION 8.4

SYNTHESIZERS ON-LINE

It's not easy keeping up with all the new developments in synthesized music. There's always new hardware, new software, new accessories, and valuable information that a lot of musicians need in order to use their electronic equipment effectively. Gary Rotger, a New York studio musician, writer, and arranger who has worked with Cyndi Lauper, Foreigner, KISS, and others, has created an on-line service called Synth-Net in an effort to establish an open forum of information, ideas, and support for synth users. The service is available as part of the IMC network (see Connection 5.5).

Rotger, who owns and operates just about every computer and every synthesizer known to man, started to document and maintain a database of information on his equipment, which is how he started Synth-Net. "It gets scary," he said, "when you buy an instrument and make a major investment, and two months later you find that another manufacturer has put something out that's cheaper and more efficient. We're catering to the professional musicians who are continuing or just beginning their MIDI education in the hopes that we can expand and exchange information and ideas."

Synth-Net is dedicated to the use, understanding and development of electronic musical instruments. Synth-Net is broken down into several areas including general interest, synth maintenance, programming, news, MIDI development, sequencing, sampling, techniques and user groups. The network encourages all its members to contribute information and ideas from their particular fields. According to Rotger, major manufacturers of musical gear, such as Oberheim, Linn, and others, will participate on the network by providing information on updates and modifications to their systems and equipment. Eventually, they'll use Synth-Net to provide on-line support to their customers. Synth-Net also tries to report from all the trade conventions, which gives members a jump on new developments.

SCREEN 1

```
  /////////////////////////////////////
  //     Welcome to SYNTH-NET (c)   //
 //    Copyright 1985 Synth-Net     //
/////////////////////////////////////
        Synth-Net Main Menu
        ******************
              Options
        D)base          F)orum
        B)ulletin       O)nline
 Hit (return) for explanation of option.
 ENTER YOUR OPTION:F
```

SCREEN 2

```
 SYNTH-NET FORUM
S)end  R)ead  SC)an  C)atagories  Q)uit

Command: C
```

SCREEN 3

```
 Available Categories:
A)Comments  B)Digidesign  C)K-MUSE
D)E-MU systems  E)LINN  F)OPCODE
G)Macusers  H)IBMusers  I)C64users
J)Sam Ash  K)Unique Recording ... etc.,etc.
Access which area: ALL

 SYNTH-NET FORUM
S)end  R)ead  SC)an  C)atagories  Q)uit

Command: R
```

SCREEN 4

```
F)wd,  B)ack,  N)ew,  O)ption: F

 System has messages:  1 to  897
    Last message read: 890

 Starting Msg * (<cr> = First): 8
```

SCREEN 5

```
Msg* 8  *Macusers* (read16times,1reply)
From:ROTTGER-US  POSTED:3-OCT-85

SUBJECT: DIGIDESIGN SOFTWARE

---MORE---

  TO ALL,
I HAVE JUST REVIEWED THE SOUND
DESIGNER SOFTWARE FROM DIGIDESIGN
AND..................................................
```

SCREEN 6

```
R)eply,  N)ext,  S)top,  or  Msg * : S

 SYNTH-NET FORUM
S)end  R)ead  SC)an  C)atagories  Q)uit

Command: Q

 Bye from Forum..............
```

Synth-Net is a service that provides on-line information and actual sound patches to music biz pros.

"Everybody is really working together on this," said Rotger. "It's very important, because somebody just getting started on a synthesizer can really get lost. No one should have to spend weeks learning to use a piece of equipment. Synthesizers are supposed to enhance and facilitate the creative process, not thwart it. The problem is that the technology moves at such a rapid pace, and it's really very hard to keep track of everything. Synthnet provides a common ground so we can all stick together and learn together."

Another on-line service in the works for synthesizer users is Synth Bank, which will provide manufacturer-supported user groups as well as high quality sound patches created by established musicians. The founder of this system is Brian Bell, who worked extensively with Herbie Hancock when MIDI was first being developed, and is now Carlos Santana's on-the-road sound engineer. Synth Bank will also be accessible via the PAN system, and Bell indicates that other on-line services may also carry the service.

One of Bell's biggest challenges in getting Synth Bank into operation has been getting the licensing agreements he needs before making artist's original sounds available via telecommunication lines. "The licensing agreements will be treated much like a record deal," said Bell. "The artist will copyright their sounds or our company will copyright it for them. The publisher will then pay them a royalty based on a percentage of sales."

For synth players who don't have modems and on-line access to the system, Bell is planning to provide in-store sound patch availability. "Synth Bank is really a wholesale company, and we plan on providing retail outlets on-line as well as inside the music stores."

How can Synth Bank's on-line sound patches be used? Bell explains: "Let's say you're working on a composition package for a film or video score and you're not trying to actually record the sound from the computer, you just want to orchestrate it and get the written music accomplished. There's no real point in spending a great deal of time making string, horn, and other orchestral sounds. So, just for a launch point, you can log onto the network and buy thirty string sounds created by one artist, and maybe twenty horn sounds created by someone else. You just download it into your home computer and have the benefit of a real sounding orchestra while you're writing your music. Why should musicians have to spend four hundred hours trying to get a good string or horn sound when they can have great sounds created by someone like Herbie Hancock or Stevie Wonder?"

The End.

APPENDIX A

A 'START ME UP' GLOSSARY OF MUSIC AND COMPUTER TERMS

Amiga: A microcomputer put out by the makers of the Commodore 64. Like the Macintosh and Atari ST, the Amiga uses the 68,000 chip as well as icons, windows, and a mouse. The outstanding features of the Amiga are its stereo sound capabilities and high resolution color graphics.

Apple II: It's really three computers: the Apple II, IIe, and IIc. When the first Apple came out it was the original personal computer, in concept and style. Things really haven't been the same since. It's still a good computer with a vast array of software. The latest incarnation may not be state-of-the-art, but it can still hold its own.

applications software: Computer programs designed to do a particular job. Word processing, speadsheets, and databases are examples of applications software. Other types of software include operating systems and program languages.

artist & repertoire (A&R): The department of a record company that traditionally is responsible for aquiring new talent. In some cases, A&R is also responsible for finding songs that an already-signed artist might record.

artist manager, personal manager: A person who professionally advises an artist on how to best package and exploit his or her talent.

Atari ST: A new computer from Atari. Sometimes called the "Jackintosh" for its similarity to the Macintosh. A very reasonably priced and powerful piece of hardware and the only computer to date to have a built-in MIDI interface.

BASIC (Beginners All-Purpose Symbolic Instruction Code): A simple computer programming language. It comes stock with most computers and allows you to write your own progams and run the thousands of public domain programs that appear in books, magazines, and on-line networks.

bit: A binary digit. The smallest unit of information a computer can deal with. A bit is either on or off (0 or 1). All digital information is represented as binary numbers.

bouncing down: A process in recording that combines the sounds on one or more tracks onto an adjacent track of the same tape to free up more space on the tape.

business manager: The person who manages an artist's money, usually for a percentage (5%-10%).

byte: Eight bits makes up a byte of information. A byte can have any value from 0 to 255 (0 to 11111111 in binary numbers). One byte, therefore, can represent any letter of the alphabet, and then some.

chart of accounts: A master list, used in bookkeeping, of all the different expense and income categories, each category is represented by a number. (i.e., 1000=accounts receivable, 1100=postage, 1200=advertising, etc.).

chip: A micro-chip. Thousands of circuits etched on a silicon wafer smaller than a penny. What used to be tons of tubes and transistors now all fits in a tiny chip.

computer language: A computer can do nothing until a program, written in a computer language, tells it what to do.

consultant: A knowledgeable expert in computers. A computer consultant can help you in deciding if you need a computer or not, and what kind of computer and software you can use to get your particular job done. A consultant should also instruct you on how to use your system and help you when you run into problems.

CPM (critical path method): A management technique for controlling and scheduling large projects.

CPU (central processing unit): A single chip that does all the computing in a microcomputer. Sometimes the whole encased unit that contains the CPU is referred to as the CPU.

CRT(cathode ray tube): The computer screen, also known as VDT (video disply terminal), or the monitor.

database: Any place that you keep information, like a phone book, a rolodex, a library, or a check book. A computer database is stored as digital information on a disk. Database is sometimes called a DBMS (database management system). The application software that allows the computer to create and work with the information that makes up the database is also called 'database'.

dedicated: Refers to a computer system, outfitted with hardware and software, that is commited to a single purpose. A word processing machine would be an example of a dedicated computer.

desk accessory: Usually a small single-function program that is always available no matter what other program the computer is running. It's called desk accessory because it is usually a phone book, clock, calendar, calculator, and other items that are found near or atop a desk.

desktop metaphor: A concept of programming that strives to create programs that mimic real life. For instance, a program that dials the phone would show a picture of a touch tone keypad on the screen and the user would select the numbers in the same way a regular phone is dialed.

digital: Representation of information in a form that a computer can understand — in bits and bytes.

digitizer: Any device that converts analog data into digital data; usually refers to a device that can take output from a video source (VCR or Camera) and convert it to a computer's screen data.

disks, disk drive: Disks are thin round platters coated with the same magnetic material as a cassette tape. Computers use disks to store and read information. Computers control the disk drives and tell it to read or write data to the disk.

There are two types of disks and drives — floppy and hard. Floppy disk drives are compact, inexpensive and portable so they can be moved from computer to computer. Hard drives are expensive, bulky, and sensitive to movement. The advantage to hard disk drives is that they hold many times the amount of data and can access it much faster.

documentation: Instructions on how to use a particular piece of hardware or software. Documentation is normally included with a purchased computer product.

double-entry bookkeeping: A standard bookkeeping method. Every transaction requires at least two separate entries — a debit and a credit. The credits must always equal the debits or you know you've made an error. Thus the term "balance the books."

drum machine: An electronic device with synthetic drum sounds capable of being programmed to play back patterns like a real drummer.

E-mail (electronic mail): The sending and receiving of written messages via a computer network.

field: Part of a database structure. A field is one unit of information like a first name, a last name, or an address. All the fields make up a record and all the records make up a file.

file: In terms of a database, a file is a particular set of records. For instance, a set of records containing names and phone numbers of clients.

file manager: A simple type of database software that can only access one file, or set of records, at a time.

flowcharting: The use of a series of lines and linking symbols to represent a succession of events. In the computer world, flowcharts are used for analysis, program maintenance, and other purposes.

freegoods: A stipulation in a recording contract that says the record company has the right to give away so many records (usually 10%) as freebies for promotion.

Gantt: A project management technique for planning, organizing, and tracking large projects.

gate: The amount of money a concert or event brings in as a result of ticket sales.

graphics: Refers to anything visible, generated by a computer, besides just plain text.

gross potential: The amount of money a concert promoter stands to make if every available seat in a facility is sold.

hard disk: see disks, disk drives

hardcopy: Computer output on paper. Print-outs.

hardware: The physical components of a computer system. Hardware is the part of the computer system that you can touch, as opposed to software which is a pattern of electrical impulses that tell the hardware what to do. Hardware is useless without software.

IBM compatible: Hardware that will accept peripherals and software designed for the IBM-PC, or software that will run on an IBM-PC or compatible machine. Compatibility is a matter of degree. Some machines are hardware compatible, some are only software compatible, and some are barely either one.

IBM-PC (The IBM Personal Computer): IBM makes four models of personal computers — IBM-PC jr., IBM-PC, IBM-XT, and the IBM-AT — all increasingly more powerful and expensive. The IBM-PC is not the most advanced micro around and certainly not the easiest to use. Because so many big corporations started computing with IBM mainframes and minis, the IBM personal computer was bound to be accepted as a business standard. So much so that a dozen or so new computer companies made millions of dollars by just copying the machine. But, with so many computer companies springing up and then disappearing, the IBM-PC was a safe choice. There are millions of IBM-PC's in use today and a multitude of software exists.

icon: A little picture on the computer screen that graphically represents an object or function. For instance, a word processing program would be represented by a picture of a typewriter or, a fuction to delete something is represented by a little trash can.

Itinerary: A list of information pertaining to each stop on a tour.

k: 1,000 bytes. 10k=10,000 bytes

laptop: A portable computer. Usually one in which the screen, disk drives (if any), and keyboard are packed into one compact unit that can sit on your lap. These computers are usually truly portable in that they run on rechargeable batteries and do not need to be plugged in.

Macintosh: Manufactured by Apple. Debuted in 1984 as the most advanced micro ever marketed and noted for its graphics and ease of use. The Macintosh was revolutionary, not just as a piece of hardware, but also for its software concepts which changed the face of personal computing on all brands of computers.

mainframe: Computers that are large enough to fill a room; many CPU's working as one. Mainframes are capable of handling huge amounts of data, which is why banks, airlines, and other businesses have been using mainframes for years.

manifest: A document containing an inventory of all the equipment being transported.

memory: A place where computers internally store information and can access it immediately. A program must reside in memory before it can be used. Information is transferred from the disk to the computer's memory and vice versa. Memory is measured in bytes and kilobytes (k). If a computer is rated as 128k, it means that its memory can hold 128,000 bytes of information at one time.

menu: A list of choices or options displayed on the screen. A menu lets you move around at will among the various functions of a program.

merchandising: The selling of merchandise with a particular act's logo or picture on it; T-shirts, buttons, bumper stickers, programs, etc.

microcomputer: A small computer based on one microprocessor. A computer that is designed to be owned and operated by one person or a small business. Micros are also referred to as "personal" computers or "small" computers.

MIDI (Musical Instrument Digital Interface): A standard agreed upon by the musical instrument manufacturers that allows instruments and computers to communicate with each other.

minicomputer: A computer with the capabilities falling somewhere between a micro and a mainframe. Mini's are as powerful as some smaller mainframes but can sit inconspicuously under a desk and, unlike a mainframe, does not require a specially designed room.

MIS (Manager of Information Services): Corporate title for the person in charge of mainframe and/or personal computers at a company.

mix down: A process in recording when many individual tracks from a multi-track recorder are blended and transferred to a two track (stereo) recorder.

modem: A device (or peripheral) that allows two computers to communicate over normal phone lines. Short for modulate/demodulate, a modem converts a computer's digital signals into audible tones (modulation) and vice versa (demodulation). How fast a modem works is measured in baud rate. A 1200 baud modem can transfer information faster than a 300 baud modem.

monitor: The computer screen, CRT or VDT.

mouse: An input device that you roll around on a flat suface and lets you point to any location on the computer screen. Move it in any direction and a pointer on the screen moves with it. A mouse will usually have a button or two that you press when you've gotten to a certain location on the screen. For many people, the mouse makes working on a computer much simpler.

MS-DOS (Microsoft Disk Operating System): The operating system used by IBM-PC's and compatibles, making it the most widely used operating system there is. Like all operating systems, it controls how information is read and written on the disk.

network: Two or more separate computers connected and able to relay data to one another; a specific set of computers (or people) linked in some way that allows access and dissemination of information. In recent years, 'networking' has become a buzz word of sorts, referring to the inter-connection of individuals for a particular purpose or business.

on-line: To be available on or to use a computer network.

operating system: A unique kind of software, sometimes called systems software, that controls the basic functions of the hardware, such as passing data to the disk drives or printer. The operating system must be running in order for any applications software (like word processing and spreadsheet programs) to function.

Optical Character Reader (OCR): An input device, sometimes called a scanner, that can read a printed page and feed the data to your computer. The U.S. Post Office uses OCR's to sort the mail.

parallel: A rating system used by the trade magazine *Radio and Records* that measures a radio station's importance in its marketplace.

personal computer: (See microcomputer).

per diem: A supplementary amount of money paid to the artists and crew for each day out on the road or in the recording studio.

personal manager: (See artist manager).

PERT (Project Evaluation and Review Technique): A project management technique for planning, organizing, and tracking large projects.

polyphonic: The capability of a keyboard instrument to produce a sound when more than one key is pressed simultaneously. For example, a chord.

printer: An output device (peripheral) that can put computer generated text and/or graphics onto paper (hardcopy). Dot Matrix, Daisy Wheel, and Laserprinters are the most popular types.

program: A set of coded instructions that tell computers what to do, written in a language that computers can understand. The program is the computer's software.

programming: The act of designing and writing programs.

publicist: A person that generates publicity for a living. A music publicist would typically hype recording acts and/or their latest product for reviews, arrange interviews, and compose press releases and bios.

publisher: A person who exploits and exposes a songwriter's musical composition.

RAM (Random Access Memory): A part of the computer's memory where programs and data are stored. RAM is "volatile" memory meaning that once the machine is turned off, the information in RAM that hasn't been saved to a disk is lost. (See memory, ROM).

record: Part of a database structure. A file is made up of records. Each record contains all the information you have concerning one person or thing in your database. For example, if you had a file containing the names and addresses of all your clients, each person is considered one record. One complete set of fields make a record. (See Field).

rider: An addendum to a contract, usually added by the performer.

road manager: The person who handles all the details and logistics of an act on tour. A road manager heads up the road crew and is usually the traveling act's primary representative if the personal manager is not around.

ROM (Read Only Memory): A part of the computer's memory which is permanent and installed at the computer factory. Usually ROM contains a portion of the operating system. ROM, as its full name implies, cannot be changed. ROM is non-volatile memory and, unlike RAM, will remain intact when the machine is shut off. (See RAM).

royalties: A percentage paid to someone based on total sales. For example, a recording artist might receive a royalty of fifty cents for each record sold. Royalties are paid in publishing, record sales, and merchandising.

scaling the house: When a concert promoter calculates what the breakdown of different ticket prices will be for a particular event.

screen: (See Monitor).

sequencer: An electronic device or computer application that will record and play back what a musician plays on one or many electronic musical instruments.

settlement: A business procedure that occurs immediately following a concert performance when the promoter and a touring artist's representative jointly calculate what monies were brought in, what deductions should be allowed, and what each party is due according to contract.

software: The program instructions written for a computer. (See Programs).

sound patch: Information analogous to a synthesizer's panel, needed to make a certain sound stored as computer data.

spreadsheet software: A software application used for calculating figures. A spreadsheet can be used for a simple column of numbers, a complex table, or anything in between.

telecommunications software: A category of application software that lets a computer, equipped with a modem, communicate with other computers via normal phone lines.

template: A ready-made form or design that a user would use in conjuction with an application software to do a specific job. For example, a spreadsheet template might have all the headings and formulas in place to do a tour budget so that all the user would have to do is enter the numbers in the appropriate places.

tour accountant: The person who controls and tracks the finances on a concert tour.

voice mail: A phone messaging system where one's voice is digitally recorded and stored in a computer system to be retrieved and played back when someone calls in to pick up messages. Also, where electronic mail messages originally typed in on a keyboard can be read back audibly over the phone by means of sophisiticated speech synthesis.

Wayne Newton: Mr. Entertainment.

windows: A software strategy that allows the computer screen to be partitioned into many sections. Each section, or window, can display a different program's data and give the illusion of having more than one computer going at the same time.

word processing: A software application used to create and edit text on the computer screen and the ability to print it out at will.

Appendix B

Quick Answers to A Few Frequently Asked Questions About Computers

Are computers smarter than I am?

No. In fact, computers are pretty stupid. They have to be told exactly what to do and how to do it. The person at the keyboard is always the boss, so there's no reason to be intimidated. A computer is nothing but a tool to help you get things done faster and easier.

How hard is it to use a computer?

That depends on the computer. The computers coming on the market now are much easier to use than their predecessors. A lot of these newer machines are designed to be more like a household/office appliance, such as a microwave oven or telephone, in that you don't know exactly how it works, but you know how to make it work for you. Using one of these new generation computers is something compared to driving a car: You don't have to know what the carburetor is to get in your car and drive to the store.

How do I buy a personal computer?

Most experts agree that the way to buy a computer is to define your needs, then find a software package that will fill those needs. Finally, buy the hardware that will run that software.

We can't urge you strongly enough: Educate yourself before you buy. Figure out what you want your computer to do for you, then make sure that such a computer exists. Talk to friends, but be careful. Friends tend to recommend the system they own. Maybe it works great for them but, then again, maybe it's the only system they've ever used. Borrow or rent a computer to get a feel for it. You might even want to take a class if you're uneasy about the investment you're about to make.

Most salespeople will not educate you. They will try to sell you the most expensive system whether or not it's what you need. Computer magazines usually publish objective articles and columns directed to the newcomer. Magazines also tend to be more knowledgeable about the latest products. There are also many fine books available (like this one). For more on magazines and books, see Appendix C.

How can I keep from buying something that's obsolete?

That's a tough one. It's almost impossible to second guess future trends in the computer industry. But even if you end up with a computer that becomes obsolete in the eyes of the manufacturer, it probably won't stop doing the work that you originally bought it for. So, don't worry about it.

How do I get the absolute "state of the art" computer?

It's the impossible dream. There's always a faster, easier, smaller, and more efficient computer coming out next year. If you decide to wait for the ultimate computer, you'll never own one.

Do I need to talk to a consultant?

A good computer consultant can set you up with just the right computer, teach you and your staff to use it, offer little tricks that are not included in the user manuals, and provide support whenever you need it. A bad consultant can recommend the wrong computer, give you lousy advice, and sell you software that was written for someone else and slightly modified to make it appear as if it was made for you. In other words, be careful. Consultants are generally expensive, but if you get a good one, it can be worth the money.

How do I choose a consultant? How do I know I'm getting a good one?

Janet Ritz is a computer consultant whose clients include Bill Graham Presents, Huey Lewis and the News, Howard Jones, George Thorogood, and CBS Records. We asked her to share with us her ten rules for picking a computer consultant. Here they are:

1. Look for a consultant with a proven track record. Ask your business associates who they have used.

2. Don't be intimidated. Write all your questions down before you meet with the consultant, then ask your questions directly. Insist on answers that you can understand.

3. Before agreeing to hire the consultant, insist that he or she give you the minimum and the maximum assessment of what your expenses will be.

4. Make sure your consultant analyzes your business requirements first and bases any software recommendations on that analysis. The consultant should then suggest the computer system most compatible with that software.

5. Once you've decided to computerize, deal with any employee and staff fears or resentment directly and immediately. Computer resistance is often an impossible environment for a consultant.

6. Don't hire a consultant just because he or she charges less than someone else. Make sure the person you hire is a specialist in the area of your needs or you could end up paying the consultant to learn on the job.

7. Shop around for the best prices on any equipment your consultant recommends. Don't assume the prices you've been quoted are competitive. Ask the consultant whether he or she receives a commission on items sold to you.

8. Insist that you get to keep all documentation that comes with any equipment, software, and specialty programs you buy.

9. Ask the consultant to write a simple "by-rote" instruction booklet with all the shortcuts and "how-to's" of the system.

10. Don't get discouraged if you've had bad experiences with a consultant. Just know when to cut your losses and find someone more qualified.

What about paying for a computer and the tax advantages?

There's no doubt about it, computers are expensive. They can be bought, rented or leased, and you should investigate all these options before jumping in. It's also important to remember that computers have a certain amount of overhead associated with them. There are always supplies to be purchased, such as printer ribbons, disks, special cleaning utensils, attachments and other occasional necessities. There are also repair bills, improvements, and upgrades to consider.

Computers may be depreciated like any other business expense, but you must keep good, accurate records on their use. You should discuss this with an accountant and find out exactly what the state and federal requirements are for tax breaks and depreciation.

Can't I lose all my data if my computer breaks down?

Not surprisingly, the most common cause of data loss or destruction is human error. Forgetting to save a file, for example, can mean hours of work down the drain. The trick here is to be careful and ALWAYS KEEP BACK-UPS! A back-up is an exact duplicate of your stored data, copied onto a second disk.

Back-up disks should be created at least once a day. Ideally, they should be stored in a different place than the original disks. In case of fire, robbery, vandalism, or a simple human mistake, you won't lose valuable information if you've followed a good back-up routine.

What is "artificial intelligence?"

This is a phrase you'll be hearing more throughout the late eighties. It is basically an area of computer science which is attempting to make computers exhibit the characteristics commonly associated with human intelligence. In other words, computer scientists are trying to get computers to be capable of "learning" and making judgments without instruction or intervention from a human being.

Despite great advances in this area, however, a computer has yet to match the amazing abilities of the human brain.

Should I buy more copies of this book to give to friends?

Yes.

APPENDIX C

Music Biz/Computer Resource and Contact List

Consultants

MacAdviser
Miles McNamara
12854 Landale Street
Studio City, CA 91604
(818) 506-5621

Martin Music Services
Janet Ritz
(415) 233-4926
IMC: RITZ-US

PSC Consultants
Paul Bugielski
2612 Carnegie Lane
Redondo Beach, CA 90278

Hardware Manufacturers

AT&T
100 Southgate Pkwy.
Morristown, NJ 07960
(201) 898-8326

Data General
4400 Computer Dr.
Westboro, MA 01580
(617) 366-8911

Epson
2780 Lomita Blvd.
Torrence, CA 90505
(213) 539-9140

Grid Systems Corp.
2535 Garcia Ave.
Mountain View, CA 94403
(415) 961-4800

Hayes Microcomputer Products, Inc
P.O. Box 105203
Atlanta, GA 30348
(404) 441-1617

Hewlett Packard
700 71st Ave.
Greely, CO 80524
(303) 350-4000

Tandy
1800 One Tandy Center
Fort Worth, TX 76102

Toshiba America
2441 Michille Dr.
Tustin, CA 92608
(714) 730-5000

Apple Computer
20525 Mariani Ave.
Cupertino, CA 95401
(408) 996-1010

Atari
Box 61657
Sunnyvale, CA 94088
(408) 745-2000

Commodore/Amiga
983 University
Los Gatos, CA 95030
(408) 395-6616

IBM Corp. Entry Systems Div.
P.O. Box 1328
Boca Raton, FL 33432
(800) 447-4700

Software Manufacturers

Apple Computer
20525 Mariani Ave.
Cupertino, CA 95401
(408) 996-1010

Ashton Tate
10150 West Jefferson Blvd.
Culver City, CA 90230
(800) 437-4329

Atari
Box 61657
Sunnyvale, CA 94088
(408) 745-2000

ATI
12638 Beatrice St.
Los Angeles, CA 90066

Batteries Included
3303 Harbor Blvd.
Suite C9
Costa Mesa, CA 92626
(714) 979-0920

Borland International
4585 Scotts Valley Dr.
Scotts Valley, CA 95066
(800) 255-8008

Commodore/Amiga
983 University
Los Gatos, CA 95030
(408) 395-6616

Dac Easy
5580 Peterson
Suite 130
Dallas, TX 75240
(214) 458-0038

Electronic Arts
2755 Campus Dr.
San Mateo, CA 94403
(415) 571-7171

Fox Productions
59 West Germantown Pike
Norristown, PA 19401
(215) 937-0347

Haba Systems, Inc
15154 Stagg St.
Van Nuys, CA 91405
(818) 901-8828

Hayden Software
600 Suffolk St.
Lowel, MA 01854
(617) 937-0200

IBM (Entry Systems Division)
P.O. Box 1328
Boca Raton, FL 33432
(800) 447-4700

Micropro
33 San Pablo Ave.
San Raphael, CA 94903

Microsoft
107000 Northup Way
Bellevue, WA 98004
(206) 828-8080

Monogram
8295 South La Cienega Blvd.
Inglewood, CA 90301
(213) 215-0529

Software Publishing Corporation/PFS
1901 Landings Drive
Mountain View, CA 94403
(415) 962-8910

MIDI

Blank Software
2442 Clay St.
San Francisco, CA 94115
(415) 922-8538

Casio
15 Gardener Rd.
Fairfeild , NJ 07006
(201) 575-7400

Cherry Lane Technologies
110 Midland Ave.
Port Chester, NY 10573
(914) 937-8601

Digidesign
920 Commercial
Palo Alto, CA 94303
(415) 494-8811

Ensoniq Corp.
263 Great Valley Pkwy.
Malvern, PA 19355
(215) 647-3930

Fairlight
2945 Westwood Blvd.
Los Angeles, CA 90064
(213) 470-6280
IMC: FINEWS

Hybrid Arts
11920 W. Olympic Blvd.
Los Angeles, CA 90064
(213) 826-3777

Kurzwiel
411 Waverly Oaks Rd.
Walthham, MA 02154
(617) 893-5900

Linn
18720 Oxnard St.
Tarzana, CA 91356
(818) 708-8131

MacroMind
1028 W. Wolfram
Chicago, IL 60657
(312) 327-3821

Mark of The Unicorn
222 3rd St.
Cambridge, MA 02142
(617) 576-2760

Music Data
8444 Wilshire Blvd.
Beverly Hills, CA 90211
(213) 655-3500

New England Digital Corp.
Box 546
White River Junction, VT 05001

Oberheim
11650 W. Olympic Blvd.
Los Angeles, CA 90064
(213) 479-4948

Opcode Systems
1040 Ramona
Palo Alto, CA 94301
(415) 321-8977

Passport Designs
625 Miramontes St.
Suite 103
Half Moon Bay, CA 94019
(415) 726-0280

RolandCorp US
7200 Dominion Circle
Los Angeles, CA 90040

Yamaha
Box 6600
Buena Park, CA 90622
(714) 522-9331

Networks

Billboard Information Network (BIN)
One Astor Plaza
1515 Broadway
New York, NY 10036

Compu-Store
777 Summer Street
Stamford, CT 6901
(800) 843-7777

Compuserve
5000 Arlington Centre Blvd.
P.O. Box 20212
Columbus, OH 43220
(800) 848-8199

Delphi
3 Blackstone Street
Cambridge, MA 02139
(617) 491-3393
(800) 544-4005
International Management Communcations (IMC)
West Coast:
183 North Martel Ave., Suite 205
Los Angeles, CA 90036
(213) 937-0347
East Coast:
254 West 54th St.
Penthouse
New York, NY 10019
(212) 757-0320

Instant Access
1020 Currie St.
Fort Worth , TX 76107
(817) 338-9444

MusicNet
P.O. Box 274
Beekman, NY 12570
(914) 724-3688

MCI Mail
Box 1001 1900 M St., NW
Washington, D.C. 20036
(800) 624-2255

NewsNet
945 Haverford Rd.
Byrne Mawr, PA 19010
(800) 345-1301

Officia Airline Guide (OAG)
(800) 323-4000
IMC:OAG
PAN
P.O. Box 162
Skippack, PA 19474
(617) 576-0862

Synth-Bank
12080 S.W. Parkway
Portland, OR 97224

The Source
1616 Anderson Road
McLean, VA 22102
(800) 336-3366

Publications

A+/Ziff Davis Publishing
One Park Ave.
New York, NY 10016
(212) 503-5147

Amiga World
80 Pine Street
Peterborough, NH 03458
(603) 924-9471

Billboard
One Astor Plaza
1515 Broadway
New York, NY 10036

Cash Box
1775 Broadway
New York, NY 10019
(212) 586-2640

Computer Music Journal
Box E
Menlo Park, CA 94026
(617) 253-2889

Hayden Publishing
10 Mullholland Dr.
Hasbrook Heights, NJ
07604

Keyboard
20085 Stevens Creek
Cupertino, CA 95014
(408) 446-1105

Microtimes/BAM
5951 Canning St.
Oakland, CA 94609
(415) 652-3810

Music Connection
6640 Sunset Blvd.
Suite 201
Hollywood, CA 90028
(213) 462-5772

Music Sound Output
220 Westbury Avenue
Carle Place, NY 11514
(516) 334-7880

Musician
31 Commercial St.
P.O. Box 701
Gloucester, MA 01930
(617) 281-3110

PC World
555 DeHara St.
San Francisco, CA 94107
(415) 861-3861

Performance
1020 Currie St.
Fort Worth, TX 76107
(817) 338-9444

Personal Computing
10 Mullholland Dr.
Hasbrook Heights, NJ 07604

Pollstar
4838 N. Blackstone Ave.
Suite A
Fresno, CA 93726.
(209) 224-2631

Related Sevices

Association of Entertainment Industry Computer Professionals
8480 Beverly Blvd.
Suite 140
Los Angeles, CA 90048
(213) 659-6010

Augie Blume & Associates/Music Industry Resources
P.O. Box 190
San Anselmo, CA 94960
(415) 457-0215

Computer-Mate
1006 Hampshire Lane
Richardson, TX 75080
(800) 527-3643

National Association of Music Merchants (NAMM)
5140 Avenida Encinas
Carlsbad, CA 92008

Quick Scan
Shel Talmy
11468 Dona Teresa
Studio City , CA 91604
(213) 650-4990

Smart Art Productions
801 6th Street
Santa Monica , CA 90403
(213) 394-5052

The Making of Start Me Up

This book was planned, researched, written, edited, composed, designed, and typeset on a personal computer.

The outline, drafts, interview transcripts, and final manuscript were word processed on Apple Macintosh 512K and 128K computers using The Word (Microsoft), Thinktank 512 (Living Video Text), and Hayden Speller (Hayden) programs.

Many of the interviews were conducted completely on-line, thus eliminating the job of transcribing them later. One interview was conducted with a consultant in London via the IMC system.

The authors verified facts and quotes with many interviewees using IMC. In fact, the only method of communication the authors had with guitarist Joe Walsh was on IMC while he was in the middle of a cross-country tour of the United States. Joe wrote the foreword for *Start Me Up* on his computer and submitted it to the authors as electronic mail.

The cover art was drawn by David Bleiman using an Amiga computer and a paint program called Deluxe Paint (Electronic Arts).

The book's layout and typesetting were done using a Macintosh 512 with a MacBottom hard disk (Personal Computer Peripherals), and page layout software called PageMaker (Aldus). Camera-ready copy was generated on the Apple Laserwriter and an Allied Linotype 300. All of the Macintosh screen images used in the book (and most of the diagrams) were included without paste-up of any kind.

ABOUT THE AUTHORS

Rod Firestone has been involved in the the record industry for more than fifteen years as a professional musician, arranger, and independent producer. As leader of the Rubber City Rebels, Rod was signed in 1980 to Capitol Records and toured extensively throughout the United States. Since then, he has written and produced a number of film soundtracks and released a record on his own label, Warner Sister Records. Over the past three years, Rod has become an expert on personal computer systems and their practical use within the music industry. He has conducted seminars and lectures and serves as an independent consultant on computers in the entertainment field.

Benjamin Krepack has been a freelance writer, editor, columnist, and West Coast correspondent for a variety of local and national music publications during the past ten years. In 1980, his interest in computers launched a second career as a technical writer, creating user guides and computer system manuals for high-tech corporations. Rather than choosing one profession over the other, Benjamin merged his two fields of expertise, writing regularly on the marriage of entertainment and technology for both music and computer magazines. In 1984, Benjamin founded Documentation Specialist Associates, a consulting firm providing technical writing and computer training services for companies and individuals in, as well as outside, the entertainment business.